Pub Strolls Around
THE YORKSHIRE
DALES

Len Markham

COUNTRYSIDE BOOKS
NEWBURY BERKSHIRE

COUNTRYSIDE BOOKS
3 Catherine Road
Newbury, Berkshire

To view our complete range of books,
please visit us at
www.countrysidebooks.co.uk

ISBN 1 85306 622 2
EAN 978 1 85306 622 1

Designed by Graham Whiteman
Photographs by the author unless
otherwise stated
Maps by Gelder design & mapping

Produced through MRM Associates Ltd., Reading
Printed by Cambridge University Press

Contents

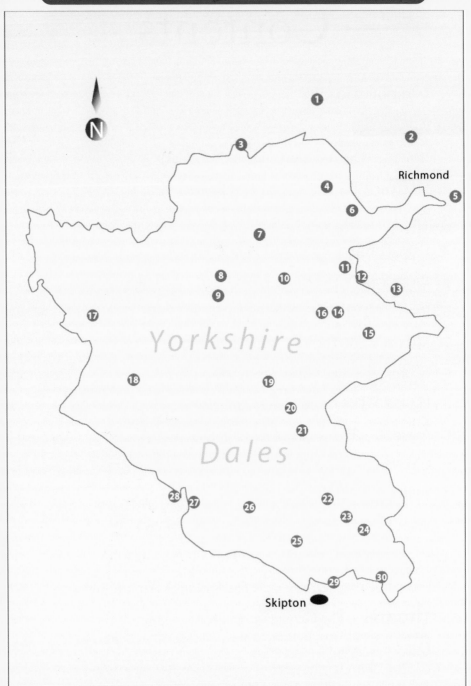

PUBLISHER'S NOTE

We hope that you obtain considerable enjoyment from this book; great care has been taken in its preparation. However, changes of landlord and actual closures are sadly not uncommon. Likewise, although at the time of publication all routes followed public rights of ways or permitted paths, diversion orders can be made and permissions withdrawn.

We cannot, of course, be held responsible for such diversion orders and any inaccuracies in the text which result from these or any other changes to the routes nor any damage which might result from walkers trespassing on private property. We are anxious though that all details covering the walks and the pubs are kept up to date and would therefore welcome information from readers which would be relevant to future editions.

The sketch maps accompanying each walk are not always to scale and are intended to guide you to the starting point and give a simple but accurate idea of the route to be taken. For those who like the benefit of detailed maps, we recommend that you arm yourself with the relevant Ordnance Survey sheet in either the Landranger or Outdoor Leisure series.

The uniquely beautiful Yorkshire Dales are known and loved the world over. With unspoilt, eye-popping landscapes, a wealth of historical interest, enough inviting inns to satisfy Bacchus and hundreds of miles of paths and trackways, the Dales offer some of the finest walking country to be found anywhere in Britain. Threaded by the demanding Pennine Way and scores of other challenging routes, the Dales offer rugged walking challenges aplenty but worn-down heels need not always equate with satisfaction. These easy to follow strolls between 1^1/$_2$ and 5^1/$_2$ miles in length give you the Dales experience without the blisters.

Many people know the area through the books of James Herriot and the internationally successful TV programme *All Creatures Great and Small* but the area has many other celebrity connections, King Richard III, Mary Queen of Scots, the artist Turner, the tightrope walker Blondin, Charles Dickens, J.B. Priestley and Kevin Costner, amongst thousands of others, all having passed this way. We will follow in the footsteps of all these people, their indelible passing adding yet another dimension to the enjoyment of this exceptional place.

Historical figures walk tall over every yard of the Yorkshire Dales, but the area has a host of other attractions – fells and purpled moors, limestone pavements with their characteristic clints and grykes, fosses and falls, potholes, drystone walls, barns, squat stone cottages that would stand the crack of doom, impregnable castles, the haunting legacy of the lead mining industry and the incomparable Three Peaks, the rearing mountain triumvirate of Ingleborough, Whernside and Penyghent, the trio overlooking Ribblehead Viaduct which carries one of the most spectacular railway lines in the world.

For convenience, all the walks start from a good pub or hotel whose telephone numbers are provided so that prospective customers can make advance enquiries about menus and opening times. Although parking details are given, walkers should always seek permission from landlords before leaving their vehicles.

Using the route descriptions allied to the sketch maps, the walks are easily undertaken, all being on public rights of way shown on the quoted Ordnance Survey Landranger and Outdoor Leisure Series maps.

With strong lungs, two stout legs and the sponsorship of my bountiful patron St Crispian, I have been triply blessed over the years, having all the equipment needed for the exploration of the incomparable Yorkshire Dales. In this my tenth walking book, it is my great joy to share with you some of my favourite Dales places . . . in colour!

Stress, we are told, is the curse of modern living. So, for this new millennium, let me prescribe the following age-old remedy for this and every other complaint, having taken the treatment for decades without any side effects:

'Walk groundly; talk profoundly; drink roundly; sleep soundly.'

Len Markham

Bowes
The Ancient Unicorn

MAP: OS LANDRANGER 92/ OUTDOOR LEISURE 30 (GR 995135)

WALK 1

DISTANCE: 2½ MILES

DIRECTIONS TO START: BOWES IS JUST OFF THE A66 BETWEEN SCOTCH CORNER AND APPLEBY. THE PROMINENT ANCIENT UNICORN IS ON THE HIGH STREET. **PARKING:** PARK IN THE INN CAR PARK OR ON-STREET.

At Yorkshire's northern frontier – I will wrestle any upstart who claims it for Durham – lofty, strategically placed Bowes has been a communications hub for centuries. The Romans built a fort here, Bowes Castle was erected for Henry II in 1171 and the famous Ancient Unicorn was the principal halt on the coaching route between York and Carlisle. The bones of generals and kings have long since vanished on the wind but the memory of one visitor remains, the names Dotheboys Hall, Wackford Squeers and Smike marking out Bowes as a literary shrine. In carrying out research for his book *Nicholas Nickleby*, Charles Dickens came to Bowes in 1838, seeking out the disreputable school which has since become a legend. Our walk follows the Dickens' trail, visiting the brooding skeletal remains of the castle and the delectable banks of the river Greta. We will discover an ancient therapeutic well along the way. Atmospheric and totally absorbing, Bowes is as impressionable as the headmaster's stick. As the walk involves crossing the Greta on stepping stones, it is not suitable after prolonged rain.

The Ancient Unicorn

Outwardly, this historic 16th century inn has changed little since Dickens 'alighted and baited' here on his journey to the Yorkshire school. Its antique portico has been enclosed and its stables have been converted to residential use but the old cobbles and the high grey gables remain, giving just an echo of the ostlers' cries and the sound of serving wenches inside. Currently undergoing progressive internal restoration to bring back the character and ambience of the old inn, the Unicorn offers intimate dining in the front parlour used by Dickens and in two separate bars, one with a yawning inglenook fireplace and a tiny cupboard used for storing tallow candles. Steaks, grilled gammon and mixed grills figure prominently in the bar menu which also includes home-made pies and fresh fish. The ale tally is Theakston, Black Sheep and John Smith's. Opening times on Monday to Friday are 12 noon to 3 pm and 6 pm to 11 pm. Weekend hours are from 12 noon to 11 pm. Telephone: 01833 628321.

The holy well beside the river Greta

The Walk

① Turn right from the inn along the street. At the far end is 'Bowes Academy' alias Dotheboys Hall. Go left between the church and the castle, following the sign, to a gate. The inspiration for Squeers – William Shaw – is buried in the churchyard.

PLACES OF INTEREST NEARBY

Bowes Museum in Barnard Castle – decorative art, ceramics, textiles, costume, archaeology and local history. Open daily. Telephone: 01833 690606. Under 3 miles west of Bowes on the A66 is the 230 acre **Otter Trust Reserve**, a breed and release facility with hides overlooking wetland areas, picnic sites and a visitor centre. Open 1st April to 31st October. Telephone: 01833 628339.

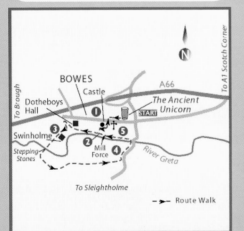

Bowes Castle

② Go through the gate (do not enter the castle enclosure unless visiting) and steer diagonally right over a field to a wall stile. Go over left and drop down left over uneven ground towards the river, swinging right and looking out for a stile to the right. Cross right into the wood and continue above the river, crossing a second stile and heading right, following a yellow arrow marker. Drop down into the dip and veer right across the flank of the hill for about 400 yards to find a ladder stile over a wall next to a lane. Cross left onto the lane.

③ Go left and swing right on the lane. Go through a gate and pass Swinholme, dropping down to the river. Cross on stepping stones and continue to a gate. Go through and walk on to the next gate, going left, following the circular walk sign and continuing on the lane for just under a mile.

④ Go left at the lane junction and walk on to cross the river bridge.

⑤ Turn left, following the footpath sign, and walk on along the river, ignoring the first path to the right. Pass the holy well and continue to a stile. Cross, continuing for 200 yards to a marker post and then go right uphill to retread the outward route. Follow the path back to the village, going right to the inn.

Dalton
The Traveller's Rest

MAP REF: OS LANDRANGER 92/ OUTDOOR LEISURE 30 (GR 115086)

WALK 2

DISTANCE: 3 MILES

DIRECTIONS TO START: DALTON IS BETWEEN RICHMOND AND BARNARD CASTLE. THE BEST ACCESS IS OFF THE A66 FROM THE A1 AT SCOTCH CORNER. GO 7 MILES ALONG THE A66 AND TURN LEFT ON A NARROW COUNTRY ROAD FOR JUST UNDER 2 MILES.
PARKING: PARK IN THE PUB CAR PARK OR 200 YARDS NORTH-EAST IN THE VILLAGE HALL CAR PARK.

The rural peace of Dalton is perversely guarded by big guns, the nearby artillery ranges on the extensive moors to the south ensuring a rare serenity amidst duvet hills. This beautifully kept, sleepy village has a century old church, an old hall where Sir Walter Scott once stayed and an Iron Age hillfort – Castle Steads. About ³/₄ mile south-west of the village, the 4 acre fort is enclosed by a stone rampart, with a deep 35 feet wide ditch. Our leafy walk over field paths and rustic tracks follows the Dalton Beck through a delightful succession of glades to the lovingly converted Dalton Mill. And there is the added bonus of a second inn conveniently placed halfway along the route.

The Traveller's Rest

This sophisticated inn does not encourage heavy armour in its car park – 'NO PARKING FOR MOD VEHICLES OVER $^3/_4$ TONNE' – but, tank crews apart, it offers visitors a warm welcome and some of the most adventurous food in the Riding. Tastefully decorated, it serves a constantly changing gourmet menu, examples including grilled goat's cheese and pine nut salad, fillet of sea bass and duck leg confit. The house ales are from the Theakston brewery. Open in the evenings only, 7 pm to 11 pm Monday to Saturday; closed all day Sunday. Telephone: 01833 621225.

The Bay Horse

At Gayle, halfway round the circuit, is the Bay Horse. Tucked snugly into a hillside, this solid, mullion-windowed, 300-year-old farmers' pub has splendid views from its twin bars. At the hub of a network of rustic lanes and footpaths, with little passing motor traffic, it is an ideal halt for walkers. Its emerald green beer garden is particularly inviting in summer. The Bay Horse serves hearty country fare such as Yorkshire pudding, steak and kidney pie, fried fresh Whitby haddock and gammon and eggs. Ales come from Cumbria's Jennings brewery. The pub is open at lunchtimes only on Saturday and Sunday 12 noon to 3 pm. Evening hours all week are 6 pm to 11 pm (7 pm to 10.30 pm Sunday.). Telephone: 01833 621468.

The Walk

① Walk forward from the inn for 150 yards and go left, following the public footpath sign through a wall gap. Cross a stile, going slightly right over a field to a gate by a bridge. Go through and turn right on a lane over the bridge, going immediately left, following a footpath sign through a farmyard. Go through a gate (arrow marker on barn upright) arcing right over the field to a second gate. Go through, keeping the same direction and heading for the trees in the middle of the field. At the next marker steer right along a hedge line, heading for an ash tree in the field corner, going slightly left to find a yellow arrow marker and a stile. Cross right and continue along the field edge for 200 yards.

② Turn right through a gate, following a blue arrow marker towards Low Fields. Walk between the farmhouse and the barn, going left at the back of the barn and swinging right to a gate. Go through and continue along Long Lane track to the road.

③ Turn right through Gayles, pass the

Bay Horse and continue for about 450 yards along the quiet lane, going left on the bend, following a footpath sign through a wall gap into a field.

④ Keep hedgeside and go through a gate, following a yellow arrow marker diagonally right across a meadow. Cross the planked bridge over a ditch into the next meadow and keep the same general direction, going to the right of a copse. Follow the next yellow arrow marker over a fence, going left, heading for the top left hand corner of the field. Go through a gate left, following the yellow arrow marker fenceside and at the next marker go through a gate right, continuing right over hummocky ground and dropping down to a pedestrian bridge over the Dalton Beck to the right of Throstle Gill. Cross the bridge and turn right.

⑤ Go through a gate into the wood and follow the beck path to Dalton Mill. Go left up the bank and continue along the access lane to a gate. Go through and turn right, back into Dalton.

Dalton Beck

Tan Hill
The Tan Hill Inn

MAP REF: OS LANDRANGER 92/
OUTDOOR LEISURE 30 (GR 897067)

WALK 3

DISTANCE: 4 MILES

DIRECTIONS TO START: EVERY ROAD TO REMOTE TAN HILL IS TORTUOUS. THE BEST ACCESS IS THROUGH ARKENGARTHDALE FROM REETH. A MORE MOUNTAINOUS ROUTE IS FROM KELD IN UPPER SWALEDALE. A THIRD EXTREMELY WINDING ROAD FROM THE NORTH LEADS FROM THE A66. THE WATCHWORDS FOR VISITING TAN HILL ARE 'WATCH THE WEATHER'. **PARKING:** PARK ON THE DESIGNATED AREAS OUTSIDE THE INN.

Tan Hill's great attraction is its coldness and ruggedness. There's nowhere else like it in the country. It surveys a wilderness of moors and peat hags, its ancient crown commanding stupendous views into the northern dales and the rock-ribbed border country to the north. The girding sea of heather once yielded coal scooped by hand from the bell pits that continue to dimple the moors but Tan Hill's abiding presence was as a refuge for travellers who plied the dour and dangerous packhorse routes between Scotland and England. One building – a buffeted island in an ocean of emptiness – dominates the heart of this Yorkshire no-man's-land, its yard-thick walls protecting the highest licensed bar in the UK. A rustic Camelot, Tan Hill has always had a profound influence on travellers and it was a frequent meeting place for important events such as funerals and boxing contests.

The Tan Hill Inn

At 1,732 feet above sea level, the Tan Hill is Britain's highest inn. Totally alone and isolated, it relies on a generator for power and large amounts of coal to keep its fires burning every day of the year. A Scott's base camp sort of an inn – beer has been known to freeze in the pipes at Tan Hill and winter at this altitude can last six months – it is extremely cosy, providing bed and breakfast accommodation and bar meals such as giant Yorkshire puddings, Cumberland sausage, hearty casseroles and a selection of filled baguettes. The meals are complemented by Theakston and John Smith's beers. In true 'been there, done that' fashion, the inn sells tee-shirts and other memorabilia. Opening times are from 11 am to 11 pm seven days a week. Telephone: 01833 628246.

PLACES OF INTEREST NEARBY

There are three spectacular waterfalls at the head of Swaledale near Keld to the south – **Wain Wath Force**, **Catrake Force** and **Kisdon Force**.

Looking towards Tan Hill Inn

Arkengarthdale (courtesy of R. Hartley)

The Walk

Other than the linear Pennine Way that passes the inn's front door, there is no formal walk around Tan Hill but you can follow the famous path for a short way or devise your own stroll, revelling in the all too rare opportunity for an unfenced and unfettered communion with nature. Come when the wind is blowing at Gale Force 6 at sea level for a really raw and exciting experience! On a clear day, however, you will enjoy every footstep.Follow the signposted path from the front door south for a 'taster' of the Pennine Way. The track leads to the eponymous Tan Hill (the site of a colliery is to the right) and on over Stonesdale Moor to Stonesdale Bridge and the minor road to Keld. Return by the same track. A trip to Keld and back on the Pennine Way would be over 8 miles.

Langthwaite
The Red Lion

DIRECTIONS TO START: AN OFFSHOOT OF SWALEDALE, LITTLE VISITED ARKENGARTHDALE IS JUST 3 MILES NORTH-WEST FROM REETH (B6270) ALONG A MINOR ROAD, LILLIPUTIAN LANGTHWAITE BEING ITS ONLY SETTLEMENT. **PARKING:** APART FROM THE ODD SPACE OR TWO THERE IS NO FORMAL PARKING OUTSIDE THE PUB OR IN LANGTHWAITE. PARK IN THE VISITORS CAR PARK 200 YARDS SOUTH-EAST OF THE VILLAGE.

Fans of the hit TV series *All Creatures Great and Small* will recognise tiny Langthwaite as the hamlet featured in the opening sequences. Occupying a rocky niche by the Arkle Beck, its handful of cottages, post office and pub could easily fit into Gulliver's palm. A busy place in the last century when the local lead mining industry was in full production, it has since reverted to growing cottage flowers and to serving walkers and cyclists who come to enjoy the peace, solitude and gritty landscapes in this tourist neglected area. Beginning by the delightful Arkle Beck, the walk leads on to the imposing Scar House before crossing meadows and climbing over rough terrain to the old lead mining grounds. Once this entire district had a working population of several thousand miners. Today, only the greening spoil heaps and the abandoned hushes and shafts are left.

The Red Lion

Diminutive like the rest of Langthwaite, this loveable urchin of a pub has a small, intimate bar decorated with photographs from its starring roles in TV and films. Despite the attentions of the BBC and Walt Disney, it is unspoilt and ethnic, serving a dual role as village pub and sweet shop. Its menu also has a traditional theme, offering substantial ploughman's lunches, lamb pie, casserole with beer and Cumberland pie, together with toasted sandwiches. The selection of ales includes Black Sheep, Theakston, John Smith's and Tetley. Opening times are 11 am to 3 pm and 7 pm (6.30 pm on Fridays and Saturdays) to 11 pm (10.30 pm on Sundays). Telephone: 01748 884218.

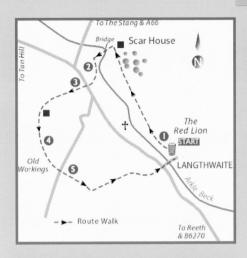

The Walk

① Go left from the pub and go left again past Stone Lea to a gate. Go through onto the beckside path and follow the distinctive waymarked route over meadows, via a succession of gates and stiles to Scar House, arcing left of the house to an access lane and a bridge over the beck. Cross and fork left past West House Cottage.

② Veer right across the meadow towards the farm cottage and go through the wall gap into the next meadow, keeping left across the meadow corner to find a second gap in the middle of the wall. Go through and turn immediately right wallside, continuing to a stile. Cross to the right of the cottage and walk on to the road.

③ Cross the road and follow the footpath sign through a gap in the wall, climbing up

Langthwaite (courtesy of R. Hartley)

on an ill-defined route over tussock grass and aiming to the right of the top cottage. Cross a planked bridge over a drain and go left at the topmost side of the cottage.

Old Gang Smelting Mill, below Healaugh Side, near Langthwaite

④ Go through two gates and merge with a rough track going through the old ore fields to the road.

⑤ Keeping the same direction, cross the road and follow the footpath sign for about 300 yards, then follow the path left between the hillocks, heading for the stand of three trees near the cottage. Join the track to the right of the cottage and follow this down, swinging left. Go through a gate to the next fork and swing left and right, going through twin gates to Langthwaite and the pub.

PLACES OF INTEREST NEARBY

Langthwaite's halcyon **church of St Mary** must be one of the most beautifully situated in the Yorkshire Dales. Approached by a broad avenue of trees from the west, it sits quietly by the Arkle Beck. Spaciously built in 1818 to receive legions of lead miners, it could today accommodate the entire population of the hamlet a hundred times over. Also worth inspecting is the equally commodious **Charles Bathurst Inn** – named after a local mine owner – ¾ mile up the valley.

Richmond
The King's Head Hotel

MAP REF: OS LANDRANGER 92 (GR 172009) **WALK 5** **DISTANCE:** 1½ MILES

DIRECTIONS TO START: THIS ANCIENT CITADEL SAUNTER BEGINS BELOW THE BATTLEMENTS IN RICHMOND'S MARKET SQUARE. THE GATEWAY TOWN TO SWALEDALE, RICHMOND IS EASILY REACHED FROM THE A1 VIA THE A6108 OR THE B6271. **PARKING:** RICHMOND CENTRE HAS DISC PARKING (FREE DISCS FROM LOCAL SHOPS).

Dramatically placed on an escarpment above the ruggedly picturesque river Swale. Richmond grew up in the shadow of one of the most impregnable fortresses in the kingdom. Guarded by steep cliffs and a series of narrow, labyrinthine bar gates, the castle, which dates from 1071, rears up like a defending sword, imposing an architectural heritage on a town that displays something of historical interest at every turn. Our walk probes the old defences, taking us along the narrow alleyways or wynds as they are known locally, through church grounds to a park by the river and on for a final assault on the curtain walls.

The King's Head Hotel

An imposing 18th century building with eight bays overlooking the market place, this elegant hotel was formerly a coaching inn whose previous guests included the famous composer Franz Liszt and the painter J.M.W. Turner. At the top of the hotel stairs is a portrait of Frances I'Anson, known as the Sweet Lass of Richmond Hill. The words of the song to her memory were composed by her sweetheart, poet and lawyer Leonard McNally, who married her in 1787. Popular with visitors, the hotel serves daily bar meals in its stylish Zetland Bar, the choices ranging from chargrilled steaks and pan fried fillet of duck to roast sea bream and Mediterranean vegetable bake. Theakston and Black Sheep beers are available in the bars. Opening times are 11 am to 11 pm on Monday to Saturday and 12 noon to 10.30 pm on Sunday. Telephone: 01748 850220.

The Walk

① Turn left from the hotel and go next left down Frenchgate. The master of Richmond School, James Tate, lived in Swale House. The young scholar Lewis Carroll had lodgings here. On the left is another interesting old house – Grove House. Built in the then fashionable brick in 1750, it was the home of Caleb Readshaw who made his brass by exporting knitted woollen caps and stockings to the Low Countries. Continue climbing on Frenchgate. Passing the house where Robert Willance once lived. In 1696, whilst out riding, he plunged over a steep cliff, upstream of Richmond. His horse died but he survived. The cliff on Whitcliffe Scar has since been known as Willances Leap. Turn right down Church Wynd.

② Enter the churchyard on a path and go next left and leave the churchyard, turning right through a gate. Go right again on Lombards Wynd to the road. Cross the road and go straight forward into the park.

③ Swing right on a broad footway above the river, following the path right and left, continuing on Park Wynd. Turn right up

PLACES OF INTEREST NEARBY

Apart from the castle which is in the care of English Heritage and is open daily – telephone: 01748 822493 – Richmond has many attractions. There are three museums in the town: the **Regimental Museum of the Green Howards** (regimental history and memorabilia), open daily except in December, no Sunday opening February, March and November, telephone: 01748 822133; the **Richmondshire Museum** (local life and industries), open Good Friday to autumn half term, telephone: 01748 825611; the **Georgian Theatre Royal Museum** (theatre history), open daily from late March to the end of October, telephone: 01748 823710.

Richmond (courtesy of B. Meadows)

the hill for 20 yards and walk up the narrow steps left to Castle Walk beneath the castle. Legend has it that a local man, Potter Thompson, discovered a cave beneath the castle. Inside, he found King Arthur and his knights sleeping soundly. They slumber on until a time when England may need their help. Swing right below the castle. The view from this vantage point hits you in the eye like a poke from a defender's halberd! Continue to the last bench before the bollards and go left down a narrow wynd to the bar. This was built in 1320.

From this eminence, you can see the tall, distinctive, octagonal Culloden Tower, erected in 1746 to rejoice in the Jacobite defeat. Go left under the bar down Cornforth Hill.

④ Turn right and walk up the steep Bargate to the top, go right on Rosemary Lane and right again down Finkle Street. (There was another bar located near the Black Lion. It was demolished in 1773.) Continue back to the market place and the hotel.

Reeth
The King's Arms

DIRECTIONS TO START: THE TOWN GREEN IS IN THE CENTRE OF REETH WHICH IS WEST OF RICHMOND ON THE B6270. **PARKING:** PARK ON AND AROUND THE EXTENSIVE GREEN (VOLUNTARY CONTRIBUTIONS FOR UPKEEP).

The capital of beautiful Swaledale is a fine market town with an independent air and solid, unpretentious stone houses encircling an expansive green. It sits confidently in the prong of the Swale and Arkle Beck, the curving backdrop of hills with names like Calver, High Carl, High Harker and Great Pinseat making you want to bolt your Yorkshire pudding and get walking! The stroll from the green takes us down to the Swale. Crossing on a pedestrian bridge, the route follows the river down to Grinton where you may visit the ancient church of St Andrews. The return track is over water meadows beside the Arkle Beck.

The King's Arms

Roaring out a welcome in winter and bright with posies in summer, the gaping inglenook of this irresistible old inn of 1734 says it all. Known locally as the 'Middle House', it offers excellent food and fine ales and the sort of relaxed, genuine and typically bluff Yorkshire atmosphere that sees pâté de fois gras happily coexist with muddy boots. Bar snacks and à la carte evening menus are available, the choice encompassing Yorkshire puddings, steak and kidney pie, fresh cod, chicken korma, poached halibut steak, trio of lamb cutlets and roast peppers stuffed with mixed vegetables. The medley of ales includes John Smith's, Black Sheep, Tetley Mild, Theakston and Timothy Taylor's supreme champion brew, Landlord. The inn is open every day from 11 am to 11 pm. Telephone: 01748 884259.

The Walk

① Turn right from the inn, pass Barclays Bank and swing right down the alley, following the sign to the river. Continue on a narrow pathway, walking between the bungalows, and turn left. Turn next right, following the sign to the swing bridge. Pass the doctors' surgery and continue on the raised flagged walkway and then on a rough track for 40 yards before turning left downhill on a path between two walls to a gate. Go through and arc right, away from the river on a footpath continuing to the footbridge. Cross left over the river and continue slightly left for about 300 yards to the Harkerside direction sign.

② Turn left along the level ground and continue to the wicket gate. Go through and keep the same direction fenceside at the bottom of a field, going left through a gate on a path wallside. Go through a gate and swing right between broken walls on a stony track to the next gate. Go through and walk on by the river, swinging right away from the bank through a gate to a quiet lane. Turn left and at the churchyard boundary go left, following the footpath sign through a gap in the wall, swinging right beside the river to Grinton. St Andrew's church to the right was built by the monks of Bridlington 900 years ago. It has many treasures – see the hagioscope, the 14th century carved font cover and the Jacobean pulpit.

③ Turn left on the footway past the Bridge Inn and cross Grinton Bridge, going immediately left, following a footpath sign through a wall gap and gate into the meadow. Go through the kissing gate and keep diagonally right across the second meadow, arcing right towards the barn and going left of it. Go through a gate, following the footpath sign to 'Reeth', and continue to the road.

Looking towards Reeth from Grinton

④ Go left, using the footway, to Reeth Bridge and cross.

⑤ Turn immediately sharp left, going left again under the arch of the bridge along the beck footpath. Go next left through two gates, following a footpath over a field and then between narrow walls, going right and left past the cottages, back into Reeth.

PLACES OF INTEREST NEARBY

Near the end of the walk is the **Swaledale Folk Museum**. It tells the story of local industry – lead mining, sheep farming, hand knitting – and fascinating displays of crafts such as drystone walling and butter making. Open every day from Good Friday to the end of October. Telephone: 01748 884373.

Muker
The Farmer's Arms

MAP REF: OS LANDRANGER 98/ OUTDOOR LEISURE 30 (GR 911978)	**WALK 7**	**DISTANCE:** 1½ MILES

DIRECTIONS TO START: MUKER IS IN HIGH SWALEDALE 9 MILES WEST OF REETH, ON THE SERPENTINE AND RATHER NARROW IN PLACES B6270. **PARKING:** ONLY LIMITED PARKING IS AVAILABLE IN FRONT OF THE PUB BUT THERE IS A PAY AND DISPLAY FACILITY BY THE BRIDGE.

Dwarfed by the imposing mass of Kisdon Hill and surrounded on all sides by lofty, poetically named fells, the hamlet of Muker recoils in its valley like some sleeping beast, its strong houses of stone and church coveting the level ground. Beside the Straw Beck whose bridge is one of the most romantic in the dale, this originally Norse settlement expanded in the days of lead mining, local people supplementing their incomes by knitting. In breathtaking scenery, unspoilt and unchanged, the village is at the hub of a number of heroic walks to Lovely Seat, Great Shunner Fell, High Seat, Nine Standards Rigg and the wild land of crags and torrents around Keld to the north. There is no finer or more inspiring walking country in the whole of England. Thankfully, those twin gatekeepers Messrs Switchback and Showers conspire to keep visitor numbers down. This wheezeless saunter along the banks of the infant Swale gives you all the grandeur of the mountains without the exhaustion. An imposing feature of this walk is the large number of traditional stone barns that seem to inhabit every field.

The Farmer's Arms

The lead mining industry originally supported three Muker pubs. Standing between rows of cottages, the sturdy Farmer's Arms is the sole survivor, its low beamed and cosy twin rooms with open fireplaces offering a traditional welcome and a range of foot restoratives that include steaks, steak pie, gammon and eggs, jumbo chicken and Stilton and vegetable crumble, jam sponge and custard and spotted dick. Bar top, the line up is Nimmos, John Smith's and Theakston Old Peculier. Opening times Monday to Saturday are 11 am to 2.30 pm and 6.30 pm to 11 pm. Sunday hours are 12 noon to 2.30 pm and 7 pm to 10.30 pm. Times may be shortened in winter. Telephone: 01748 886297.

The Walk

① Go left from the pub and left again by the church, swinging left and right to find a footpath sign 'To Keld'. Follow a track past the vicarage and continue, going uphill

On the fells above Muker (courtesy of D. Lewis)

Muker (courtesy of B. Meadows)

at the bend. Continue forward through the gates into a wood and proceed in the same direction, going through further gates. Drop down right to a barn. Arc sharp right to the Ramps Holme footbridge along the river bank to a wicket gate.

② Go through right, following the sign to 'Muker', walking along a distinctive flagged footway through a series of gated wall gaps. Head for the church tower, arcing right, back into Muker.

PLACES OF INTEREST NEARBY

St Mary the Virgin church dating from 1580. Its most fascinating feature is its east window, the pastoral background representing the scenery around Muker – the Swale, the Straw Beck, Kisdon Hill and local fellside walls.

On the wall of the **old school** left of the pub are two fading memorial plaques to former pupils. Richard Kearton was a naturalist, author and lecturer (1862–1928); his brother was a naturalist, author, explorer and a pioneer of wildlife photography (1871–1940).

Hardraw
The Green Dragon

| MAP REF: OS LANDRANGER 98/ OUTDOOR LEISURE 30 (GR 867913) | WALK 8 | DISTANCE: 3¼ MILES (INCLUDING FALLS VISIT) |

DIRECTIONS TO START: TAKE THE A684 NORTH-WEST FROM HAWES FOR ABOUT 1½ MILES, GO THROUGH APPERSETT, CROSS NEW BRIDGE AND TURN FIRST RIGHT ON A MINOR ROAD TO REACH THE HAMLET OF HARDRAW. **PARKING:** PARK IN THE INN CAR PARK OR ON-STREET.

The tiny settlement of Hardraw is situated at the foot of Abbotside Common in a sylvan spot overlooking the Fossdale Gill, its epic geology and a unique natural wonder having drawn visitors for centuries. Falling a hundred feet in one plunge Hardraw Force is one of the most spectacular waterfalls in the country. In Victorian times, its acoustics were found to be ideal for brass band competitions and championships were held in its natural amphitheatre. The annual event still continues. Hardraw's reputation also attracted the attention of the Great Blondin. He walked across the chasm on a tight rope while cooking an omelette!

Using a spooky old miners' track on a plateau at the edge of the moor, we pass Yorkshire's very own Easter Island idols, strange families of cairns thrusting up like sea stacks with their stone siblings. Dropping down to a delightful dell path by the gill, this stroll of contrasting sights, sounds and earthy smells then enjoys the cascading tinkle of ivories before the crescendo of that mighty leap.

The Green Dragon

Guarding its watery lair hard by the bridge over Fossdale Gill, this gritty old inn retains its Yorkshire range and open fireplace, its ambience and hearty menu welcoming tired legs and large appetites, the typical menu including meat and potato pie, chicken, lentil and vegetable bake, steak pie in ale and fillet of salmon with caper sauce. The dragon's tipple is exclusively Theakston – Bitter, XB and Old Peculier. Opening times Monday to Saturday are 11 am to 11 pm. Sunday hours are 12 noon to 10.30 pm. Telephone: 01969 667392.

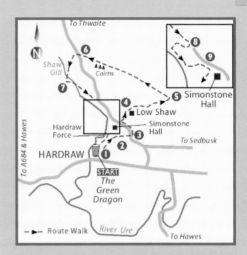

The Walk

① Turn left from the inn and go immediately left, following the footpath sign to 'Simonstone', through a gate and over a courtyard and up steps. Continue forward into a field wallside on flagstones, gradually veering away from the wall right on a rising, cobbled way in the direction of a copse and a house. Climb steps and weave left to a stile. Cross left and climb more steps into a second field and swing right at the side of the house to the signpost and go through the gated wall gap on the right.

② Go forward over a meadow on the flagged path and go through a gated wall gap by a barn. Continue wallside in the next field, passing in front of Simonstone Hall Hotel and swinging right to a wall gap. Go through left and turn right on the access drive, continuing to the lane.

③ Turn left on the lane, passing the back of the hotel, and continue for 150 yards. Turn right on the access drive to Low Shaw, climbing up, passing the bungalows and going left of the barns on the concrete hardstanding, arcing right at the back of the barns and then left uphill fieldside to a gate.

④ Go through into a second field, heading towards a barn, and swing right to a gate. Continue through into a third field, steering left towards a copse and a wall corner (there is a large sycamore in the wall apex). Go left here, following the wall up to a stile. Cross and keep forward through the bracken, climbing up and right heading towards a clump of trees (the path is indeterminate at this point). Continue forking right to the foot of the shales and climb up to find a cairn and plateau track.

⑤ Turn left on the level track, passing the successive lines of cairns, and follow the wall down towards the lane, dropping down left and going through a wall gap by a gate. Swing right on a green track and drop down left through bracken to a ladder stile. Cross to the lane.

⑥ Turn right along the lane for 100 yards.

Hardraw Force

PLACES OF INTEREST NEARBY
In nearby Hawes is the **Dales Countryside Museum** depicting Dales life from 10,000 BC to the present day. Open daily from Easter to the end of October. Telephone: 01969 667450.

Fork left, following a footpath sign to 'High Shaw ½ mile'. Walk to the right of a barn, turn briefly left, then turn right over a ladder stile and left downhill, wallside. Cross a stile at the field bottom, enter the edge of a wood by the gill and cross a second stile, continuing for 100 yards.

⑦ Go left over a stile into a field and follow the middle path, swinging right between the top two trees and over a stream, going through a gated wall gap to a second field, then continuing over the field to another gated wall gap. Go through to High Shaw and turn right, following the footpath sign between the outbuildings to a lane.

⑧ Turn sharp right for 150 yards. Turn left through a wall gap down a ladder to the gillside path and go left, passing a number of cascades, using the flagged path. Beguilded by the big drop, most tourists miss this wonderful spot. Look out for kingfishers and rare ferns. Go through the gate by the bridge and keep left, swinging left to the lane.

⑨ Turn right along the lane for 200 yards to the Low Shaw access and go right, following the footpath sign at the side of Simonstone Hall over a stile and through a gate and dropping down right to the right of a barn to the outward route. Retrace your steps back to the inn.

Entry to Hardraw Force is via the inn and a small fee is payable.

Hawes
The Board Hotel

MAP REF: OS LANDRANGER 98 OUTDOOR LEISURE 30 (GR 872899)

WALK 9

DISTANCE: 2 MILES

DIRECTIONS TO START: MAKE YOUR WAY TO THE CENTRE OF HAWES WHICH IS ON THE A684 AT THE HEAD OF WENSLEYDALE. **PARKING:** PARK ON STREET OR IN THE PAY AND DISPLAY CAR PARK OFF HARDRAW ROAD TO THE EAST OF THE TOWN.

Encircled by grand fells, bustling Hawes takes its name from the word 'hals', meaning a pass between mountains. Formerly a rugged 'sack o' beans and bushel of flour' sort of a place filled with shops selling sheep dip, cattle medicines and milk pails, it is now firmly a haunt of tourists, hosts of tea rooms, cafés and pubs gracing its streets, although the traditional old industries of rope and cheese making continue to flourish.

This short amble along part of the Pennine Way through meadows, takes us to the picturesque sister settlement of Gayle, although there was no kindred love lost here. Until the Great War, for some reason lost in time, a simmering feud existed between the people of Hawes and Gayle and there were many bare knuckle fights. Now the much painted hamlet, with a pretty beck bridge and narrow alleys with quaint names like Marridales, Beckstones, Garris and Thundering Lane, is peace itself. Although poor, Gayle was the most famous centre in Wensleydale for the hand knitting of gloves, caps and jerseys, the old cottage industry going back to the 16th century and surviving here longer than anywhere else. To save fuel, women and children would 'go a-sitting', gathering in each other's homes round a peat fire with their needles telling ghost stories. The men of Gayle were generally employed as wallers or drainers.

The Board Hotel

Wafting homely smells into the Market Place with a menu as genuine as grandma's apron, the dapper and very popular Board Hotel offers a wholesome range of meals including roasted lamb shoulder marinated in mint and honey, Wensleydale coddled chicken, gammon and eggs and local sausage. It has adjoining twin bars decorated with photographs showing local crafts and scenes. The house ales are Tetley, Theakston, Black Sheep and Calders. Opening times Monday to Sunday are 11 am to 4 pm and 6 pm to 11 pm. On Tuesdays the hotel is open from 11 am to 11 pm. Telephone: 01969 667223.

The Walk

① Turn left from the hotel along the street and fork right to the church. Turn right into the churchyard and go right by the entrance door to a gate, going through

Lane near Hawes (courtesy of R. Hartley)

to a path. A large church, St. Margaret's was built in 1851 at a cost of £2,300. Turn left and go through a wall gap, forking right on a causeway, following a footpath sign alongside the Gayle Beck. Go through a second wall gap and swing right at the back of the creamery, going through two gates to the road. Turn left along the footway for 100 yards.

② Turn right, following the 'Pennine Way' sign at the side of a bus shelter, between the houses. Cross the back lane, keeping straight forward, and go through a wicket gate and left over a field to a second wicket gate. Go through and cross a small field to a third wicket gate, going through to a lane.

③ Turn right on the lane, following the 'Pennine Way' sign, and follow the lane left, right and left uphill to the tall, small barn. Turn right along the lane to the junction.

④ Turn left at the junction and walk on to the Gaudy Lane junctions on the right, keep going forward for a further 40 yards.

⑤ Turn left through a gated wall gap into a field and continue through a second gated wall gap into a second field. Walk on to another wall gap, go through into a third field and (ignoring the Pennine Way sign) go diagonally left towards the church tower, dropping down left to a metal kissing gate. Go through and down steps, turning right into Gayle and weaving left to the road and the bridge to your right. The view upstream is a favourite subject for artists. Nearby is a three storey mill built in 1784 for producing cotton.

⑥ Turn left and rejoin the outward route, retracing your steps back to Hawes and the hotel.

Askrigg
The King's Arms

MAP REF: OS LANDRANGER 98/ OUTDOOR LEISURE 30 (GR 948911)

WALK 10

DISTANCE: 3 MILES

DIRECTIONS TO START: ASKRIGG IS NORTH OF THE A684 NEAR BAINBRIDGE.
PARKING: PARK ON-STREET.

An attractive town from every point of the compass, 'fells roll back from it and meadows creep up to it', Askrigg was once the centre of the local lead mining, knitting and clock making industries, more timepieces being produced here than anywhere else in the North Riding. A thoroughly absorbing and rumbustious place, years ahead of its time, it devised a novel method for relieving male angst. If a man wanted to expel his frustrations in a fight he would turn over the town's bull ring, another belligerent turning it back to accept the challenge. The town also had a colourful Hill Fair, vividly described in a poem of 1847:

Stallions proud with ribbons prancing,
Joyous fiddling and dancing.

Issac Horsfield who was there,
He made sport for all the fair.

A handsome show of china ware,
Of much variety was there.

Cheese-cakes plenty might be got,
Ginger bread and good tom-trot.

This stroll through fields to the hamlet of Newbiggin and Nappa Scar revels in some of the stirring history of the area.

The King's Arms

Built around 1767, the historic King's Arms, near the church, has three atmospheric rooms sprouting a menagerie of stuffed animals and every conceivable old implement and tool, its display of photographs revealing a more theatrical past. This glorious example of the English pub in all its warmth and quirkiness – it has roaring open fires in winter and real soot! – was chosen as the setting for the 'Drovers Arms' in the hit TV series *All Creatures Great and Small*. It serves a wide selection of bar snacks such as steak and ale pie, rib-eye steak, ham and mushroom pie, pan fried venison and fresh fish. The selection of ales includes Theakston XB and Black Bull, Old Speckled Hen and John Smith's. Opening times Monday to Saturday are 12 noon to 3 pm and 6.30 pm to 11 pm. Sunday hours are 12 noon to 3 pm and 7 pm to 10.30 pm. Telephone: 01969 650258.

The Walk

① Turn left from the inn along the street, arcing left, and go left again on a lane signposted 'Muker'. Part ascend the 1 in 4 hill, walking past Hargill House on the left, and go right opposite Lee Gate, following a footpath sign through a gated wall gap.

② Follow the wall down over a field and swing left to a gap by a gate. Go through into a second field, veering left to a gap by a gate. Go through, continuing on a path between walls, swinging left and right over a beck into Newbiggin – which must have the distinction of possessing the tiniest village green in the country.

③ Go to the left of the green between the cottages and go through a gate, keeping wallside, and walk over this first field and then cross five more fields in the same general direction, using gates/wall gaps. In the seventh field, veer left to a gated wall gap and go through into the eighth field, steering left to the field corner. Go through the gated wall gap into the ninth field steering diagonally right to the wall corner and a barn, keeping the same general direction, crossing the tenth and eleventh fields through gated wall gaps. Go through a wall gap in the twelfth field and turn right, following the wall down to the hamlet of Nappa Scar. Continue to the road and turn left.

④ Walk down the road for 200 yards and

PLACES OF INTEREST NEARBY

St Oswald's church, near the inn, is said to be the biggest and stateliest in Wensleydale. It has an interesting connection with this walk, in that the south chapel was founded in 1468 by James Metcalfe of Nappa Hall, the last of his direct descendants being buried there in 1756.

Nappa Hall

swing right into the Nappa Hall entrance downhill.

⑤ Swing left and turn right on the track, passing the hall. This is really a fortified manor house, consisting of two towers with a hall between. It was bestowed on James Metcalfe who sent a hundred Yorkshire Archers to Agincourt in 1415. So prominent were the Metcalfes in the 16th century that 300 family members, all on white steeds, attended Sir Christopher Metcalfe when he was made High Sheriff of Yorkshire in 1556. Another resident – Sir Thomas Metcalfe who was colourfully known as the 'Black Knight' – laid seige to Raydale House, near Semerwater, in 1671, after a feud with his neighbours. Several people were wounded and two were killed in the conflict which is regarded as the last act of domestic warfare in the country. Mary Queen of Scots was allowed to visit Nappa Hall whilst a prisoner at nearby Bolton Castle. Continue for 150 yards and go right through a gate, following a footpath sign, going left across a field to a second gate. Go through and left over the next field towards a barn, climbing a stile and going through a gate on the right to the lane.

⑥ Turn right on the quiet Low Gate Lane uphill, continuing to the road.

⑦ Swing left at the junction into Askrigg, go left again round the bend and right back to the inn.

Carperby
The Wheatsheaf

DIRECTIONS TO START: CARPERBY IS BEST REACHED FROM THE A684 IN AYSGARTH. TAKE THE MINOR ROAD NORTH OVER THE RIVER FOR ABOUT ½ MILE AND GO RIGHT AT THE CROSSROADS TO COME TO THE WHEATSHEAF ON YOUR LEFT. **PARKING:** PARK EITHER IN FRONT OR BEHIND THE INN – OTHER SPACES ON-STREET.

Carperby's restrained prettiness reflects its sober past as a centre of Quakerism. At the foot of a steep fell, the Friends Meeting House of 1864 stands proud amidst lines of cottages, some bearing 17th century date marks on their lintels. On the green and around the prominent village cross which is raised on steps, a market was once held, Carperby being credited with breeding the first Wensleydale sheep in 1838. Our stroll takes us over a mosaic of walled fields, whose boundaries have hardly changed in a millennium, to the world famous Aysgarth Falls. This spectacular and supremely picturesque succession of cataracts on the Ure has attracted numerous artists and photographers over the years; the set-to between 'Robin Hood Prince of Thieves' and Little John was also filmed here. Following the river through Freeholders Wood, the route takes in the high, middle and lower falls before returning on an old lane to Carperby.

The Wheatsheaf

A long-established Yorkshire inn whose previous guests included Greta Garbo and James Herriot, who spent part of his honeymoon here in 1941, the inviting stone-built Wheatsheaf has an attractive bar, an adjacent snug and a small but intimate restaurant. Popular with locals and visitors alike, it stills serves – by candlelight! – that time-honoured Yorkshire favourite ham and eggs, together with a range of mainly traditional dishes such as giant Yorkshire puddings with various fillings, smoked haddock with dill sauce, lamb hotpot and steak and bacon pie. The house ales are Webster's, Black Sheep, Theakston and John Smith's. Opening times vary according to the season and passing trade but are generally 12 noon to 3 pm and 7 pm to 11 pm (10.30 pm on Sundays). Telephone: 01969 663216.

The Walk

① Follow the Aysgarth footpath sign directly opposite the inn, going through a gate into a field. Go right through a second gate into a field and turn left, following a wall down for 100 yards to a signpost. Turn right to find a gate in the field corner and go through, walking over two further fields using the wall gaps. Turn left wallside down a long, narrow third field to a wall gap. Go through onto Low Lane and turn right to the road.

② Go left using the verge for 50 yards and fork right across the road, going through a wall gap, following the sign to Aysgarth. Walk parallel with the road over the first field, go through a wall gap into the second field, veering away from the road right and keeping to the right of the metal fenced copse to find a stile. Cross into a third field, heading towards the wood, and negotiate a gated stile entering the wood, dropping down to a kissing gate. Go through, keeping right and dropping down left to a second kissing gate. Go through and drop down steps to the car park. Turn right, following the sign to the Upper Falls along the path to the bridge (originally erected in 1539 as a packhorse bridge). Veer right along the river bank to the falls and return to the car park.

③ Follow the footpath sign forward to the Lower Falls, crossing over the car park to the left of the Visitor Centre and take the signed footpath to the Middle and Lower Falls, crossing the road right and going left into Freeholders Wood. Renowned for its hazelnuts, this is the only remaining fragment of the ancient Forest of Wensleydale of any size. Follow the distinctive path, visit the Middle Falls to the right and keep on the path, going through a gate to the Lower Falls, visiting and returning to the path. Go through a

Carperby (courtesy of R. Hartley)

PLACES OF INTEREST NEARBY

Overlooking Aysgarth Falls, housed in an old mill, is the **Yorkshire Carriage Museum** whose displays include 57 Victorian coaches. Open daily all year. Telephone: 01969 663399.

gate and keep forward on the path, swinging right to a further gate. Go through and you will come to a stile and a signpost marked 'FP Castle Bolton'. Go left over the stile into a field and swing right, following a fence down to a gated wall gap and a sign marked 'Redmire and Castle Bolton'. Go through and over a field to the underside of the barns at Hollins House, going through a gate and swinging right on the farm access road.

④ Swing left on the track, ignoring the footpath sign to the right, keeping left over the cattle grid and the route of the abandoned railway, going through a gate to Low Lane. Walk on to a point about 200 yards past the farmhouse on the left to the signpost marked 'Carperby Village'.

⑤ Turn right through a gated wall gap into a field, steering left through the broken wall gap over the next field to the outward signpost, retracing your steps back to the inn.

Redmire
The Bolton Arms

<table>
<tr><td>MAP REF: OS LANDRANGER 98/
OUTDOOR LEISURE 30 (GR 045913)</td><td>WALK 12</td><td>DISTANCE: 2¼ MILES</td></tr>
</table>

DIRECTIONS TO START: REDMIRE LIES WEST OF LEYBURN. THE BEST ACCESS IS FROM
THE A684 IN WENSLEY VILLAGE, GOING NORTH-WEST FOR ABOUT 4 MILES.
PARKING: PARKING IS LIMITED OUTSIDE THE INN. ALTERNATIVE PARKING ON HARGILL
LANE (NORTH OF THE INN) NEAR THE RAILWAY BRIDGE.

With crow's nest views, bonny Redmire looks serenely out on Wensleydale, its flowered cottages, ancient green and church snug in the gaze of a towering sentinel to the rear. A former lead mining settlement whose name derives from the reeded lake that once occupied the low land at the south of the village, Redmire is dominated by the shivering towers of Bolton Castle, a remarkable, largely preserved fortress, which has been described as a climax of English military architecture. Misbehave in the medieval precincts, and its impact is so real and of the moment that, just for a second, you might imagine a crossbow bolt zinging past your ear.

Our walk over tracks that may well have been used by the desperate Mary Queen of Scots who fled incarceration in the castle in 1568 takes us alongside the track of an old railway line and through fields to the village of Castle Bolton.

The Bolton Arms

This light and airy, cherubic little inn has an inviting lounge with a log burning stove and a small dining room, both serving a medley of traditional bar meals, the menu typically including liver and onions, roast shoulder of lamb, plaice stuffed with prawns and a local speciality – lample pie (lamb, apple and mint). The ale options are Black Sheep, John Smith's and Theakston. Opening times are Monday (closed lunchtime) 6.30 pm to 11 pm, Tuesday to Saturday 12 noon to 2.30 pm and 6.30 pm to 11 pm and Sunday 12 noon to 3 pm and 7 pm to 10.30 pm. Telephone: 01969 624336.

The Walk

① Turn left from the inn along Hargill Lane and walk on uphill towards the railway bridge. Go under the bridge and turn immediately left, following the footpath sign.

② Cross the footbridge over the Apedale Beck and continue walking straight

PLACES OF INTEREST NEARBY

Bolton Castle has a shop and a café and is open daily from March to November. In winter by appointment. Telephone: 01969 623981.

forward parallel with the embankment. Swing right across a footbridge over a ditch, arcing away from the embankment over a field, heading to the left of a barn. In the field corner, go through a gated wall gap and steer left over the next field, heading towards Bolton Castle. Go through a second wall gap and proceed over the bottom of the field towards the castle, negotiating a third wall gap, then turn sharp right, following the line of a wall towards a gate. Go through the wall gap to the right of the gate and continue on the track into Castle Bolton. Turn left to the castle. Such is the shock and utter power of what is undoubtedly one of the finest castles in Europe, that all your attention will be drawn to the towers above you and you should allow plenty of time for visiting the castle and its grounds. Begun in 1379 by Sir Richard Scrope, Lord Chancellor of England at the time of Richard II, the fortress has a wealth of chambers and rooms to explore, dark corridors, spiral staircases and cobbled court-yards adding to the excitement that culminates for many in a visit to Mary Queen of Scots' Bed Chamber. The current occupant of the castle, who can trace his ancestry back to the first Lord Scrope, has, despite the seemingly overwhelming martial presence of the castle, created a relaxing family home.

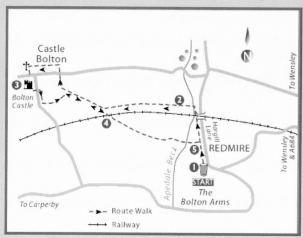

41

Bolton Castle

Perhaps it's the children's toys in the courtyard, the herb garden and vineyard against the battlements or the wonderfully tended garden to the south.

③ Having explored the castle, turn right downhill and walk south along the quiet lane, going left on the bend, following the footpath sign over a stile, continuing between drystone walls. Swing left and go through a gate, keeping left over the long field to the third of the previously negotiated outward wall gaps. Go through right and make your way back to the embankment.

④ Cross the embankment, forking right, go through a gap in a fence and cross a field left, using the stepping stones over boggy ground to find a gate. Go through and forward to a stile. Cross and go immediately left through a wall gap, following the wall down to a fence. Go through the gap and cross the Apedale Beck on the stepping stones. Go through a wall gap and cross a meadow to another wall gap, going through and weaving left over a field at the back of the cottages. Swing right to a stile and cross, continuing on a track to Hargill Lane.

⑤ Turn right down the lane, back to the inn.

Wensley
The Three Horseshoes

DIRECTIONS TO START: WENSLEY IS ON THE A684 JUST OVER A MILE SOUTH-WEST OF THE MARKET TOWN OF LEYBURN. **PARKING:** PARK IN THE INN CAR PARK OR ON THE PARKING AREA NEAR THE CHURCH.

Wensley village gives its name to the whole glorious dale and there are more evocative descriptions of Wensleydale's views, waterfalls, castles, abbeys and pretty hamlets than you can throw a thesaurus at. Wensley itself, an estate village tied to Bolton Hall, lies on the banks of the incomparably beautiful river Ure – peer in its pools and you will instantly become a brother of the angle. It consists of no more than a few cottages, a church and a wonderful little pub. Long by stroll standards but well worth doing, this epic walk takes us over pastures and through the market town of Leyburn to the soaring limestone scar of Leyburn Shawl, a poignant place of history where the fleeing Mary Queen of Scots was captured after her escape from Bolton Castle in 1568. The return route is over meadows and through the fields of Wensley Park.

The Three Horseshoes

Flower-smothered in summer with twin fires up its chimney backs during the colder months, this joyful little inn has two homely, low-beamed rooms and a lovely sunny terrace, its wholesome, zestful menu smacking of fresh ingredients and an obvious pride in the kitchen – booking advisable. Choose from an exciting menu that includes Dales lamb, pan fried duck breasts, smoked chicken served with a tangy fruit glaze and pistachio nuts, sea scallops sauteed in burgundy or an authentic 'Dales Plateful' – a platter of sliced chicken and Yorkshire ham, spiced sausage and Wensleydale cheese. The complementary ales are Theakston, Black Sheep and John Smith's. Opening times Monday to Saturday are 12 noon to 2.30 pm and 5 pm (7 pm in winter) to 11 pm. Sunday hours are 12 noon to 2.30 pm and 7 pm to 10.30 pm. Telephone: 01969 622327.

The Walk

① Go left from the inn downhill towards the church. Dating from 1245, this is full of treasures – a famous Flemish brass, many armorial shields and a fine Bolton pew. Turn left on Low Lane and go left again after 150 yards, following the arrow marker past Glebe Cottage. Swing right uphill and just before Rectory Garth, go through the second gate on the right, following the arrow marker left across a small field. Cross a stile, veering right across the second field and dropping down in the field bottom towards a power post. Keep going forward to a stile, crossing into a third field. Stay fenceside to the corner and go left uphill at the edge of a copse. Go right over a stile, following the arrow marker, and go right over another stile into Old Glebe Field Nature Reserve and then left wallside. Keep going in the same general direction, crossing ten more fields using stiles and wall gaps until you come to a barn.

② A few yards on, turn left, following an arrow marker over a stile and keeping fieldside to the corner. Go right across a stile and continue along the long meadow, going to the right of the ash tree in the corner and crossing two ladder stiles to the railway line. Cross and weave right and left to a third ladder stile. Cross and go right over a field to a gap in the wall, crossing into the second field and going right to the road. Turn right on the footway into Leyburn.

③ In Leyburn, walk towards the Bolton Arms, going right of it down Commercial

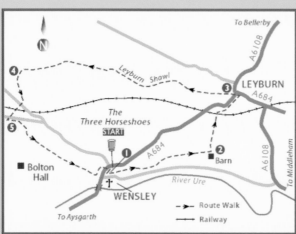

44

Looking towards Penhill from Wensley

Square. Weave right, left and right, following the sign and going through two gates to The Shawl. Proceed straight forward through a series of wall gaps and over three fields, continuing on a woodland path and following the ridge path as it swings right. Keep wallside, following the arrow marker, and enter the wood, continuing on the well defined path for about ¹/₂ mile. Drop down left to a stile. Cross left over a field and at the second stile, fork right to the smallest of the hawthorn trees and cross a third stile, keeping the same direction to a fourth stile, heading down the long field and bearing left to the corner.

④ Go left on the track, following the yellow arrow marker through a gate. Pass the farm buildings to the left and drop down left and right and left again to the road. Cross and go through a gate, following a footpath sign over a small field. Cross a stile to the railway line. Cross the line. Go through a gate, following the arrow marker and steering right across a field. Go through a further gate to the lane.

⑤ Turn left for 250 yards and go right, following a footpath sign into a wood. Turn left after 50 yards on a track, bearing right and left fieldside. Go left at the 'PRIVATE' sign and walk on in an arc right and enter a large field, walking in the direction of a big central oak tree, weaving left and right to the Bolton Hall access road. Continue through Wensley Park to the A684 and go left, back to the inn.

PLACES OF INTEREST NEARBY

Bolton Castle is 5 miles north-west (see Walk 12). Just across the valley from Wensley, **Middleham Castle**, the childhood home of Richard III, is open daily from March to October; Wednesday to Sunday in winter. Telephone: 01969 623899. Beyond Middleham along the A6108 is the **Brymor Ice Cream Parlour** – 30 flavours. Telephone: 01677 460377.

West Burton
The Fox and Hounds

DIRECTIONS TO START: WEST BURTON LIES SOUTH OF THE A684 LEYBURN-HAWES
ROAD (TAKE THE B6160 EAST OF AYSGARTH AND THEN A MINOR ROAD).
PARKING: PARK AROUND THE SPACIOUS GREEN.

Set in a necklace of sweet fells, West Burton has been described as the best village in the whole of Wensleydale, its spacious green alive with the babble of children, its dapper old houses and cottage gardens and its attractive waterfalls on the Walden Beck giving it great charm. At the junction of Bishopdale and Waldendale and surrounded by the turret heights of Penhill, Naughtberry Hill and the mighty Addleborough, it was once an important market town. Today it earns a living from agriculture and tourism, its tranquillity protected by the boon of twin 'no through roads'.

In scenes of reckless beauty, this elevated pastures orbit gives us just a peep of Waldendale. We skirt the foot of Walden Moor whose crest is marked by the site of an ancient settlement and field system and linger by the cool vapours of the Walden Beck waterfall.

The Fox and Hounds

Overlooking the green, this white-washed, part stone-flagged, unassuming pub is as hospitable as a cottage parlour, its rustic menu offering traditional ham and eggs, steaks and daily specials such as Stilton and broccoli quiche and fisherman's pie. A free house, its wide range of ales includes Theakston, Black Sheep, John Smith's and Webster's. Opening times during the summer months are from 11 am to 11 pm daily. Reduced hours in winter. Telephone: 01969 663279.

The Walk

① Go right from the pub and pass the school and West Burton House, continuing on a track towards the farm.

② Go left on a stony track before the farm, swinging left, right and left again to the quiet lane.

③ Turn right along the lane for 200 yards and go left through a gated wall gap, following a footpath sign to 'Cote Bridge ¹/₂ mile'. In the field, keep to the right of an electricity pole, dropping down on the bank, and go left at the footpath sign over a footbridge spanning the Walden Beck.

Falls on the Walden Beck

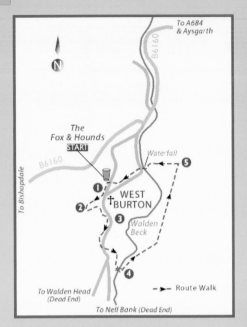

gap and continue past Riddings to the next gated wall gap. Go through two more fields and gated wall gaps, and in the third field ignore the track left downhill but fork right instead to find a gated wall gap, going through and dropping down to the footpath sign.

④ Turn diagonally left over a meadow, following the footpath sign to 'Riddings', and cross a ladder stile over a wall, continuing over a field and through a gate, keeping left wallside for 150 yards and going left through the gated wall gap. Steer right over a field, go through a gated wall

⑤ Follow the footpath sign and the wall left, and go through the gated wall gap to the left of the barn, dropping down left through a gate and down steps to the falls. Swing right and left over the bridge, going right again by the cottages and then left, back into West Burton.

Carlton-in-Coverdale
The Forester's Arms

DIRECTIONS TO START: CARLTON, ONE OF A NUMBER OF SIMILARLY NAMED VILLAGES IN YORKSHIRE, IS IN COVERDALE, ITS VALLEY LINKING WENSLEYDALE WITH WHARFEDALE. THE EASIEST ACCESS IS FROM THE A6108 AT MIDDLEHAM, GOING SOUTH-WEST ON COVERHAM LANE. **PARKING:** PARK OUTSIDE THE INN.

The ancient glaciers conspired a luscious torpor for the little visited valley of the Cover, the magnet of Wensleydale deflecting most cars along the line of the river Ure to the north. With remains of the old abbey at Coverham and evocative reminders of the days of coaches, packhorses and lead mining, at just 12 miles long, Coverdale sleeps on unmolested by traffic, its broad canvas of pastures and wide fells guarded by the imposing heights of Dead Mans Hill and Great Whernside. Amazingly though, the road up the valley was once the coach route from London to Richmond. In the centre of the dale, Carlton once presided over the 'courts of the forest' and it is thought that an ancient parliament was held here to settle disputes. And according to the Middleham accounts of 1465–67, Carlton had a common oven, a corn mill and a brewery. Circling the river, this stroll takes us through fields towards the village of West Scrafton where the writer James Herriot spent many holidays.

The Forester's Arms

This beautifully presented, classically English inn, would have had members of the Pickwick Club clammering for seats on the Yorkshire coach. Stone-flagged and low-beamed with open fireplaces and bright with flowers and gleaming brass, it has appealing twin bars and a superb restaurant. Stuffed with sporting trophies, prints and bottles of vintage port, this added evening attraction has the intimacy of a gentleman's study. An award winning inn, the Forester's presents an adventurous menu offering everything from chargrilled wood pigeon and fillet of roast ling with parma ham and a butter sauce perfumed with coriander to traditional sausage and mash and venison casserole. Matching the versatility of the main menu is a list of cheeses, the selection including the locally produced Coverdale. The house ales are John Smith's, Theakston, Black Sheep and a guest. Daily opening times are 12 noon to 3 pm and 6.30 pm to 11 pm (10.30 pm on Sundays). Closed on Mondays in winter. Telephone: 01969 640272.

The Walk

① Go left from the inn along the road for 250 yards. Turn left, following the footpath to 'Flats Hill', steering left to the gated wall gap. Go through and continue forward over six fields, using the wall gaps, to the lane.

② Turn immediately left, going through a gate, following the sign to 'Cover Lane'. Cross a field and head for a middle wall, crossing to the left of a gate. Cross and continue to the right of a barn and go

through a gated wall gap, following the wall down to the 'FP Carlton' sign, going through the wall gap to the lane.

③ Turn left down the lane, walk round the bend and over the river Cover and Nathwaite Bridge, climbing uphill for 300 yards. The river Cover is a delectable and boisterous mountain stream that rushes from its watershed between Buckden Pike and Great Whernside. It holds good heads of trout and grayling and although shallow and difficult to fish, it is the delight of anglers. Charles Kingsley fished here and wrote: 'Little Cover in his deep wooded glen with his yellow rock and bright white stones and brown water clearer than crystal'.

PLACES OF INTEREST NEARBY

Back along the Coverham road, in the Tupgill Park Estate, is the remarkable **Forbidden Corner** – an eccentric and bizarre collection of strange statues and follies that combine the creepiness of the ghost train with the puzzlement of a maze. Open Good Friday to the end of October but prior telephoning is advisable: 01969 640638.

A leafy lane near Carlton-in-Coverdale

④ Turn left, following a footpath sign 'FP West Scrafton'. Do not continue straight forward here – enter the field but go immediately right through a gate into a field and then aim right, away from the Cover valley towards a fragment of wall. Go through and continue fenceside, veering right and left to the footpath sign on top of the mound and fork left, following the sign to 'Caygill Bridge'.

⑤ Head downhill towards the trees, weave left and go through a gate, continuing fenceside beside the gill. Swing left to a bridge. Cross and bear right across the second, smaller footbridge and go through a gate, swinging right and left around the base of the mini hill, following the footpath sign uphill. Follow the line of hawthorns, then veer right across a field, following the line of the wall down towards a barn. Go through a gate left.

⑥ Walk down a track between two walls, continuing between the cottages to the road. Turn left, back to the inn.

Thoralby
The George

MAP REF: OS LANDRANGER 98/ OUTDOOR LEISURE 30 (GR 999868)

WALK 16

DISTANCE: 4½ MILES

DIRECTIONS TO START: THORALBY IS BEST REACHED FROM THE B6160 – THE ONLY ROAD UP BISHOPDALE – COMING OFF THE A684 JUST EAST OF AYSGARTH.
PARKING: PARK IN THE SMALL CAR PARK TO THE FRONT OF THE INN OR ON THE LANE.

Like snaking tree rings, Bishopdale's contours are deeply compressed between the heights of Naughtberry Hill and Stake Fell, in just five miles the lonely valley of the Bishopdale Beck falling nearly 900 feet to Thoralby. A retiring village, its name means 'Thorold's Farm', it is set under the hill on the 'sunny side of the valley' – the settlement of Newbiggin on the opposite slope is said to be on 'the money side' – Thoralby has been spruced up in recent years, some of its neat old cottages providing accommodation for the few fortunate tourists who either by design or an aberration of the compass venture this far. This reasonably taxing but rewarding walk, some of it over rough ground, follows a steady climbing track to the grouse butts on Heck Brow. With panoramic views of nearly half of Wensleydale, it descends on a parallel route back to Thoralby. This is not an outing for the gregarious. Normally only the lone Pacific mariner experiences this much solitude.

The George

Smart in a livery of white paint and flowers, this beguiling, homely and thoroughly relaxing little inn has everything but your fireside slippers, its reputation drawing discerning visitors from far and wide to tackle a menu that would bring a smile to any cowman's cheek – typically beef casserole cooked in ale or steak and kidney pie in addition to salmon and broccoli mornay. The ale choice is Black Sheep, Webster's and John Smith's. Opening times Monday to Saturday are 12 noon to 2.30 pm (closed Monday lunch-time) and 6.30 pm to 11 pm. Sunday hours are 7 pm to 10.30 pm. Telephone: 01969 663256.

The Walk

① Starting at the George, turn right on the lane for 300 yards then go right at the signpost marked 'Busk Lane 4 Aysgarth 1¼'. Climb steeply up the track, going right and left, walk on, passing Swinacote Gill to your left, and swing right and left, crossing Hasker Gill Beck. Keep climbing and go through a gate, continuing onto the moorland, following a green track. Go through a second gate and follow the wall down, swinging right and left, walking up and to the left of Gayle Ing – the prominent copse and farmhouse to your right. Go through a third gate and continue up to the rise, walking on and swinging right for a further 250 yards. There are few reference points here but the grouse butts to the left over a wall – accessed by a paving slab stile – should help to fix your position. Simply but effectively made from rough timber and tufts of ling, the grouse butts

Bishopdale

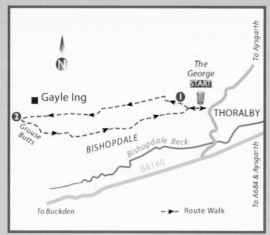

A farmhouse in Bishopdale (courtesy of B. Meadows)

② Turn sharp left through the tussock grass on a faint path running parallel with the drystone wall. Cross the line of a broken wall, following the path towards the wall corner, and swing right at the corner, continuing on a line parallel with the wall, and gradually veer away left from the wall and the beck, heading back down the Bishopdale valley. Veer right to a gate, go through and steer right at the edge of the tussock grass, dropping downhill and merging with a broken wall. Walk to the bridleway sign and continue wallside, going through a gate to the second direction sign. Go right, following the bridleway, and left over a stream bed, forking right to a third sign and arcing left, following the track marked 'PW Thoralby'. Go through a series of gates and take the left fork, keeping the gill to your right, and continue on the lane, passing Old Hall (date stone 1641), back to the inn.

PLACES OF INTEREST NEARBY
At the west end of the village is a house marked with the initials MS and a date stone of 1704. Local legend says that treasure is buried here. An old man once dreamt that he saw a black teapot stuffed with gold sovereigns under the floor. From time to time, flagstones have been removed in an, as yet, futile search.

melt into the landscape. Overall, this outward stretch of the walk is about 2¼ miles.

Dent
The Sun

MAP REF: OS LANDRANGER 98/ OUTDOOR LEISURE 2 (GR 705870)

WALK 17

DISTANCE: 2 MILES

DIRECTIONS TO START: THE VILLAGE OF DENT IS REACHED BY NARROW AND WINDING MINOR ROADS, EITHER FROM THE A684 AT SEDBERGH IN THE NORTH-WEST OR FROM THE B6255 AT GAYLE MOOR IN THE SOUTH-EAST. **PARKING:** PARK IN THE INN CAR PARK OR IN THE LARGE PAY AND DISPLAY FACILITY TO THE NORTH-WEST OF THE CHURCH.

Shoe-horned into the serpentine valley of the Dee, just two main routes access this remarkable village in the western Dales. Motoring here can be an epic adventure, ending with doubts as your vehicle bounces over chariot-wide cobbled streets, wondering if this place has been lost for years. Such isolation – Dent's own railway station is a perverse four miles distant – has nurtured a proud independence down the years, the village once being one of the most important centres in the Dales for hand knitting. Dent has another claim to fame. Adam Sedgwick, the famous geologist, was born here in 1785. This Cambridge Professor of Geology is commemorated by an inscribed granite monolith in the main street.

With long distance fell views, this totally relaxing and uncomplicated stroll takes us along the banks of the river Dee, returning over water meadows to Dent.

The Sun

Reflecting its namesake, this splendid, early 16th century inn has dazzling white walls and the cheeriest of signs to attract the dourest abstainers, low beams, open fireplaces, a home-spun menu and real ale brewed nearby, combining to create one of the most appealing little inns in the Dales. Special recipe steak and kidney pie heads the list of dining options, the choice including a good selection of vegetarian dishes such as roast vegetables gratin and Brie courgette crumble. The house ales – as individualistic as a Dent sock but twice as warming – are, in order of potency, Dent, Aviator, Kamikaze and T'Owd Tup. Opening times Monday to Saturday are 11 am to 3 pm and 6 pm to 11 pm. Sunday hours are 12 noon to 10.30 pm. Telephone: 015396 25208.

The Walk

① Turn left from the inn over the cobbled alley for 30 yards and go right past Church Gate Cottage into the church grounds, dropping down steps to the right of the church. Originally Norman, St Andrew's

Dent (courtesy of R. Hartley)

Dent Head Viaduct (courtesy of B. Meadows)

was last restored in 1889. Leave the churchyard and go left on the road, dropping down to the Dee bridge.

② Go right over a stile, following a path signed to 'Middle Bridge' over a field, and then turn left through a metal gate over a stream bridge by the ruined barn, crossing a stile and continuing on a raised footpath between two fields, wallside. Follow the banks of the Dee right and upstream and cross a series of stiles to the footbridge.

③ Turn right on what appears at first glance to be the dry bed of a stream, following this sunken path and continuing to a gate. Go through and swing right on Double Croft Lane.

④ Swing left past Double Croft and go through a gate and swing right to a further gate. Go through and follow the hedge line down, arcing left and following a stream bank at the side of a meadow. Cross a ditch using a stile and planked bridge, going left and right towards the neck of a narrow field. Go through a wall gap and keep along the beck bank, going through a gated wall gap and then left over a bridge and through the gate to regain the outward path. Retrace your steps back to the inn.

PLACES OF INTEREST NEARBY

The access road from the south-east passes two dramatic Settle–Carlisle railway viaducts – **Dent Head** and **Artengill**. By way of a real treat, if you take the train from Settle or Ribblehead, you can appreciate both these marvellous structures in style, alighting at Dent Station and then getting a taxi to the village. For timetable details, telephone 08706 023322.

Ribblehead
The Station Inn

<table>
<tr><td>MAP REF: OS LANDRANGER 98/
OUTDOOR LEISURE 2 (GR 764792)</td><td>WALK 18</td><td>DISTANCE: 2¾ MILES</td></tr>
</table>

DIRECTIONS TO START: THE STATION INN IS AT RIBBLEHEAD NEAR THE RAILWAY STATION AND THE B6255/B6479 JUNCTION. **PARKING:** PARK OUTSIDE THE INN OR ON THE EXTENSIVE GRASS VERGES NEAR THE JUNCTION.

Seared into the map with the force of a branding iron by the railway pioneers who created the legend that is the Settle-Carlisle, the name Ribblehead has the resonance of a hot rivet. Consisting only of scattered farmhouses, a railway station and an inn, the hamlet is located slap-bang in the middle of Three Peaks Country, the famous summits of Penygent, Whernside and Ingleborough casting their spells from every direction. Under 2,500 feet they may be, but when the clouds blow hot over Black Shiver Moss, show me a meaner brood of mountains and I'll eat my hat . . . if I can find it.

This stroll take us first to the 24-arch marvel that is Ribblehead Viaduct. Completed in 1871 at the cost of many lives, it is the centrepiece of the 72 mile long Settle-Carlisle line which penetrates some of the most magnificent scenery in England. At the foot of Whernside, we wander towards Blea Moor signal box – this is the terrestrial equivalent of lighthouse keeping – passing under the line and returning by Batty Green. Deserted now, this wilderness attracted men and women from every part of the kingdom. Nowadays we can stand at leisure and glory in the views in every direction.

The Station Inn

Is this the only inn in England having its own railway station? Aptly named, this refuelling stop for the Three Peaks Walk is a sort of reverse oasis, travellers sometimes coming here to remedy the effects of *too* much water. Stoutly built and cosy with bar and dining room options serving mainly Yorkshire staples such as steak and ale pie, lamb's liver and onions and fresh cod and chips, the Station also offers a popular bunk barn service for ramblers. The ale choice is Black Sheep and Theakston. Opening times Monday to Friday are 11 am to 4 pm and 6.30 pm to 11 pm. Saturday opening is 11 am to 11 pm. To cater for early morning walkers, Sunday opening is from 9 am to 3 pm and 6.30 pm to 10.30 pm Telephone: 015242 41274.

The Walk

① Turn left from the inn along the road for 100 yards. Go left, following the bridleway sign, on a pathway and swing left under the viaduct on the broad track. The 72 miles of track cost £47,500 per mile – an astronomical sum for the 1870s. The costliest portion of all was the Ribblesdale to Eden Vale section. Blea Moor tunnel

The Ribblehead Viaduct

beyond Ribblehead averaged £45 per yard. Some of the pier foundations of the Ribblehead viaduct are 25 feet deep; its total length is 1,320 feet. Swing right and left again, going through a gate, then going right to the barns at Gunnerfleet Farm. Go through a second gate, cross the bridge over the Winterscales Beck and turn right.

② Follow the beck using the track, swinging left by the hillock to a gate. Go through to the track junction.

③ Turn right following the sign to 'Deepdale 5¹/₂' on a path, crossing a stile by a cattle grid. Continue on a lane and just beyond Winterscales Farm, go right following the 'FP Whernside' sign over a humped back bridge on a rough track, going through a gate and heading left towards the signal box. Swing right to the

PLACES OF INTEREST NEARBY

In constructing the Settle-Carlisle line, hundreds of people died from injuries, overwork, malnutrition and cholera. You can see a memorial to the workers and their families down the road from Ribblehead in the cemetery of Chapel-le-Dale church.

tunnel and go through under the railway line.

④ Turn right alongside the railway line on a broad track and continue to a stile, crossing and dropping down steps to the left of the viaduct. Keep left over Batty Green to the road.

⑤ Turn right along the road, back to the inn.

Hubberholme
The George

MAP REF: OS LANDRANGER 98/ OUTDOOR LEISURE 30 (GR 927783)

WALK 19

DISTANCE: 3½ MILES

DIRECTIONS TO START: THE BEST ACCESS TO THE TINY UPPER WHARFEDALE VILLAGE OF HUBBERHOLME IS ALONG THE B6160 BETWEEN GRASSINGTON AND THE A684 NEAR AYSGARTH. TURN OFF WESTWARDS BETWEEN BUCKDEN AND CRAY. **PARKING:** PARK IN THE INN CAR PARK.

An incantation, as soft as a sigh, the name Langstrothdale will linger long in the memory of a visit to this hidden valley of the Wharfe – a blithesome river – unspoilt, unsullied and totally unforgettable. In 1933, the novelist and playwright J.B. Priestley came here. Hubberholme has changed little since his car chugged up the dale, and the inn where he stopped for lunch '. . . they gave us soup, Yorkshire pudding, roast chicken, fruit pudding, cheese and biscuits, and coffee, all for two and sixpence each . . .' is still here. In a deeply carved valley, the hamlet consists of no more than the old inn, a scattering of farmsteads, several old cottages and the beautifully situated church of St Michael. Wild flower meadows and ancient woodland clothe the valley sides that rise abruptly to the sky, against the light a triumphant group of fir trees standing out like some martial standard. Our stroll ascends the hill to the evocative Scar House. In 1652, George Fox, the founder of the Quakers, converted its owner who established a Friends Meeting House here. Through woodland, the path leads to Yockenthwaite – in old Norse 'Eogan's Clearing' – returning alongside the river accompanied by a Yorkshire mascot – the dipper.

The George

Set in a nook by the Gill Beck, this whitewashed cocoon has walls as thick as breakwaters and splendid fireplaces. A former farmhouse and vicarage, it has mullioned windows, twin flagstoned bars and a collection of locally caught glass-cased trout that will have you forgetting your thirst and rushing out for the fly box. Its typical menu includes baked goat's cheese, mushroom and leek pie, salmon and haddock pie, marinated lamb in beer and lamb chops. The George serves Tetley and Black Sheep ales. The inn is open every day from 12 noon to 3 pm and 6.30 pm to 11 pm. Telephone: 01756 760223.

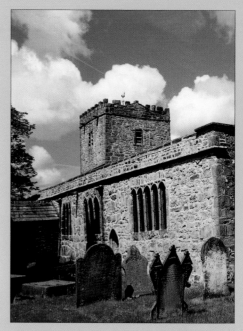

Hubberholme's 12th-century church (courtesy of A. Holubecki)

The Walk

① Cross the bridge from the inn and swing right of the church, going left through a gate, following a sign to 'Yockenthwaite'. Take the right fork signposted to Scar House uphill. Climb up the winding track and cross the ladder stile by the National Trust sign and weave up right to Scar House, dated 1698. To the side of the house, which is now a National Trust holiday cottage, is a small enclosure dotted with five trees. This was a former burial ground although there are no headstones.

② Walk to the left of the house, looking out for the yellow arrow marker on the side of a barn, and go right, following this marker, at the back of the house, swinging left to the signpost and continuing for 100 yards to the 'FP Yockenthwaite' sign. Turn left here through a gated wall gap and weave left to the top of the tree line, following the path right, entering a wood through a wicket gate. Cross a rustic bridge, dropping down left and continuing on the track through two wall gaps. Keep

Hubberholme (courtesy of B. Meadows)

going forward on the distinctive path, crossing three broken walls and then going through a wall gap, a gate and a further broken wall, continuing beyond the barn. Go left, following a footpath downhill, heading towards the bridge in the bottom. Follow the footpath sign right on a narrow track, go through a wicket gate and continue, going through a gate and left on a track downhill towards Yockenthwaite and a footpath sign. At the farmhouse, go left, following the 'Hubberholme' sign. A few hundred yards further upstream to your right on the public footpath is a stone circle.

③ Swing right to the lower gate to the 'FP Hubberholme' sign and go left through this and two more gates, swinging right to a wall gap. Go through and down steps and follow the footpath sign left along the river bank. Continue on the distinctive footpath over a succession of gated and stiled fields back to Hubberholme and turn right, back to the inn.

PLACES OF INTEREST NEARBY

The magical Norman **church of St Michael**. 'Very rough interior' says the Pevsner guidebook. See it! Inside is an inscription to J.B. Priestley whose ashes are scattered nearby. 'He loved the Dales and found Hubberholme was one of the smallest and pleasantest places in the world.'

Starbotton
The Fox and Hounds

<table>
<tr><td>MAP REF: OS LANDRANGER 98/
OUTDOOR LEISURE 30 (GR 953748)</td><td>WALK 20</td><td>DISTANCE: 4 MILES</td></tr>
</table>

DIRECTIONS TO START: STARBOTTON LIES ON THE B6160 NORTH OF GRASSINGTON, BETWEEN KETTLEWELL AND BUCKDEN. **PARKING:** PARK IN THE INN CAR PARK.

With its pretty skirts neatly tucked in, Starbotton's circle of houses lies in the glacial U-shaped valley of the Wharfe at a point where the Cam Gill Beck finally makes a break for freedom from its oozy moor. Lead mining has been carried on in this area since the 17th century and in 1843 ore was smelted in Starbotton Cupola, its snaking flue running over 1,000 feet up the hill to a chimney in Cam Pastures. Today, just a few spoil heaps and abandoned chimneys and tunnels remain, the scars only adding to the lonely and desolate grandeur of a succession of evocatively-named moors. Up a precipitous path, I will lead you to Knuckle Bone Pasture on a track that is humorously called a road, to the foot of Starbotton Fell and the site of the old workings. You will then have the experience of a Yorkshire speciality, the route leading through a quaking, peaty blancmange. The path has wonderful views but it is indistinct in places and this stroll is best reserved for fine days.

The Fox and Hounds

This is one of the cosiest little inns in the entire Dales, with its open fireplaces, freshly made Yorkshire puddings and soufflés, old fashioned crusty pies, robust roasts and championship ales. It has a stone-flagged bar with window seats and a collection of old pots and a small adjacent dining room, the imaginative menu also offering dishes like chicken and leek crumble, bacon steaks with orange and mushroom and lamb cooked with apricots. The ales are from the award-winning Timothy Taylor brewery together with Black Sheep and Theakston. The inn is closed all day Monday. Tuesday to Saturday opening is from 11.30 am to 3 pm and 6.30 pm to 11 pm. Sundays hours are 12 noon to 3 pm and 7 pm to 10.30 pm. Telephone: 01756 760269.

The Walk

① Turn right from the inn along the lane and turn left by the bench, walking on a few yards and swinging sharp right uphill on a track, following the signpost to 'Out Moor'. Climb up to the next signpost and take the right fork, marked 'BW Walden Head'. Continue climbing, going through a succession of gate openings on a well-defined track for around 1¹/₄ miles, heading up towards the head of the valley. At the bridleway sign, keep going forward and gradually swing right towards the valley head, passing the spoil heap to your right, up to the cairn. Some 50 yards after the cairn, swing right.

② Follow the arcing track at the head of the valley right, proceeding through a succession of gates and gate gaps, heading away from the line of the valley, and then go right parallel with the line of Out Moor Top to the left. Continue to the old tips

The valley of the Cam Gill Beck

PLACES OF INTEREST NEARBY

The local woodlands, hillsides and hay meadows are a haven for rare flowers including cowslip, yellow rattle, betony, bistort, eyebright, greater butterfly orchid, melancholy thistle and wild thyme. During the Second World War a war-plane crashed here in a blizzard, killing most of its crew. A Polish survivor crawled to safety through the snow fields following footprints of a fox to a farmhouse. The flyer and the fox are commemorated in a memorial on the summit of Buckden Pike.

swollen Cam Gill Beck obliterated many of Starbotton's old cottages. (The angle of the track is much less pronounced than that shown on the OS map.) Merge with a green track and cross a stile, dropping down and swinging hard right and left to a more substantial track.

③ Turn sharp right on this track between drystone walls, heading directly towards the valley.

④ Turn left downhill, swinging right and left on a snaking track to a stile. Cross and go left on a track, turning right into Starbotton and left on the lane back to the inn.

and swing right to the cairn and follow the track parallel with the Cam Gill Beck valley to the right, gradually arcing right. After a fearful storm in 1686, the heavily

The village of Starbotton, looking towards the Fox and Hounds pub. (courtesy of B. Meadows)

Kettlewell
The Racehorses

DIRECTIONS TO START: THE VILLAGE OF KETTLEWELL IS NORTH OF GRASSINGTON ON THE B6160. **PARKING:** IN THE INN CAR PARK OR NEAR THE RIVER BRIDGE – FEE PAYABLE.

Kettlewell captivated my attention when I was still in school plimsolls. Even before I came to the village I used to read its contours on the old 1 inch OS map like some pals read *Boys Own*. A rugged and beautiful place, it is a sort of Heathrow for walkers and cyclists; tracks, paths and the Yorkshire Dales Cycleway whizzing off in every direction. And the airport allusion is quite apt, the surrounding hills of Great Whernside, Buckden Pike and Old Cote Moor Top rising to dizzy heights. And watch the vapour trails of the cyclists coming down Park Rash! For centuries, Kettlewell was a busy market centre. At the hub of a network of packhorse routes it had thirteen pubs, only three of which remain. A popular haunt of students who come to study the classical form of the Wharfe's glacier-carved valley, it is alive in all seasons with the ritual garment zippering before the grunting starts. But there need be no panting on this flat walk of polished gate hooks and catches, our route following the river bank to the hamlet of Starbotton and back.

The Racehorses

This handsome hostelry is strategically placed between the Cam Beck and the river Wharfe and passing customers readily fall to its charms. An 18th century former coaching inn, it sits beside the beck bridge with meadow views to the rear. Attractive and inviting, it has a central bar with an open fireplace date-stoned 1640 and a large back room. Its good choice of lunchtime dining options includes giant Yorkshire puddings, steak and ale pie, curry of the day, fresh haddock and vegetable lasagne. More substantial evening meals are available in the restaurant. The tally of beers is Theakston, John Smith's and guests. Opening times Monday to Saturday are 11 am to 11 pm. Sunday hours are 12 noon to 3 pm and 7 pm to 10.30 pm. Telephone: 01756 760233.

The Walk

① From the inn, fork left on the lane passing the village hall and walk up to the 'FP Starbotton' sign and follow this sign uphill, climbing to a wicket gate. At a gearbox crunching 1 in 4, Park Rash just up

The Wharfe valley between Kettlewell and Starbotton

PLACES OF INTEREST NEARBY

Just south of Kettlewell, along the B6160, is the famous rocky overhang known as Kilnsey Crag. A few hundred yards from here is **Kilnsey Park and Trout Farm**. This family attraction has fly fishing, a children's adventure centre and an estate shop and delicatessen specialising in Dales produce. Open every day. Telephone: 01756 752150.

and follow the additional signposts through a succession of gates into Starbotton.

② Cross the road and keep going straight forward, following the 'FP Kettlewell 2' sign, dropping down on a track between walls to the river. The Wharfe has a sprinkling of trout and kingfishers are quite common hereabouts. Cross the river on a footbridge and go left, following the 'FP Kettlewell' sign. Follow the very distinctive and well-signposted path through a series of gates and wall openings, crossing a number of stiles to Kettlewell. Swing right opposite the back of the Racehorses to the bridge and go through a gate, cross the bridge left and walk back to the inn.

the hill, is reckoned to be one of the most severe stretches of road in England. Go through and after 20 yards, go left, following the distinctive path for about 1$^3/_4$ miles above the valley, running parallel with the river. At the footpath sign, go left

Kettlewell (courtesy of B. Meadows)

Grassington
The Black Horse

MAP REF: OS LANDRANGER 98/
OUTDOOR LEISURE 2 (GR 003641)

WALK 22

DISTANCE: 2½ MILES

DIRECTIONS TO START: GRASSINGTON CAN BE REACHED ON THE B6265 BETWEEN PATELEY BRIDGE AND SKIPTON OR ON THE B6160 NORTH FROM ILKLEY. THE INN IS IN THE VILLAGE CENTRE, JUST OFF THE MARKET SQUARE. **PARKING:** CAR PARKING IN THE SQUARE IS LIMITED BETWEEN 9 AM AND 5 PM TO ONE HOUR. LONG STAY PAY AND DISPLAY PARKING IS AVAILABLE JUST 5 MINUTES WALK FROM THE SQUARE IN THE NATIONAL PARK VISITOR CENTRE ON HEBDEN ROAD.

This 'Gateway to Upper Wharfedale' is a crowded, craggy town of tall buildings and dark yards set into the hillside overlooking Yorkshire's finest river. Despite the genteel tourist shops and smart restaurants, like many a dour dalesman it presents a bluff and gritty face mirroring the surrounding countryside – an enigmatic wilderness of rocks, abandoned medieval villages, field systems and the legacy of an extensive lead mining industry. The extraction of lead just a few miles up the road at Yarnbury at the edge of Grassington Moor once occupied hundreds of men.

This short stroll – serene and pacific, it's like the best cruise liners – is the preferred solace of Grassington residents who want a respite from the tourists! Passing by Tom Lee's old forge it takes a back lane to the river and the beauty spot of Ghaistrill's Strid. Following the river, it leads to the picturesque Linton Falls beside an old mill, returning along a quiet track through the Visitor Centre grounds and by back alleys to the square.

The Black Horse

With its stout quoins, rearing black and white façade and plain no-nonsense sign, this imposing old coaching inn has the gaunt look of a lead mine foreman eyeing a latecomer. But climb the steps, cross the little courtyard and do not be intimidated! Inside, the scowl vanishes in the discovery of a rich seam complemented by an open fireplace and a cosmopolitan list of meals. Another popular retreat of Grassingtonians, the immensely friendly Black Horse has a traditional bar and extensive eating areas including the Stables restaurant serving a varied menu including baked gammon steak, chicken curry, broccoli and Stilton quiche, seafood platter and roast duckling. The house ales are Theakston, Black Sheep, John Smith's and Tetley. Opening times on Monday to Saturday are 11 am to 11 pm. Sunday hours are 12 noon to 3 pm and 7 pm to 10.30 pm. Telephone: 01756 752770.

The Walk

① From the inn walk into the square and turn right and right again on the lane going uphill past Tom Lee's old blacksmith's shop (now a florist's) In 1766, the foul deeds of Tom Lee came to national attention with the discovery of the murdered body of a local doctor in nearby Grass Wood. Lee was executed in York and his body was gibbeted in what is now a nature reserve. Pass the library and turn left down Chapel Street. Pass the Methodist church and at the junction with Bank Lane sweep left downhill, swinging right on the lane to the junction with Grass Wood Lane.

② Turn right along this lane for 50 yards and go left, following the 'FP River Wharfe' sign on a track, swinging right

The River Wharfe (courtesy of D. Cossar)

The packhorse bridge in Linton (courtesy of B. Meadows)

towards a barn. Go through a gate and turn left at the barn to a fence and a wall corner. Go left through the wall gap and follow the wall down to the river.

③ About turn at the rocks and go left along the riverside path towards the bridge, gradually bearing left and going through a kissing gate to the road. The packhorse bridge was erected in 1603. Although most bridges over the Wharfe have at one time or another been washed away by floods, this proud structure has remained undamaged.

④ Cross the road and go left for 20 yards and then right, following the sign 'FP Hebden and Burnsall'. Continue along the river bank and cross a footbridge over a stream, swinging left past the first weir to the second weir.

⑤ Go through a wall gap and follow the

PLACES OF INTEREST NEARBY

Take the dead-end road north-east from Grassington, signposted to Yarnbury, to view some of the best preserved lead mining industry remains in the country. Information boards point out the main features. In Grassington's square, housed in two former lead miners' cottages, is the **Upper Wharfedale Museum** depicting local life. Open daily from Easter to mid-October; weekends only the rest of the year (no telephone number).

path left, signposted 'To Grassington Village', on a causeway. Continue and go left through a gate into the National Park Centre, crossing to Hebden Road.

⑥ Cross the road and go left, turning right up Springfield Road. Go left at the hammer-head and turn right on the path. Go next left and weave left back to the square and the inn.

Burnsall
The Red Lion

| MAP REF: OS LANDRANGER 98/ OUTDOOR LEISURE 2 (GR 033613) | WALK 23 | DISTANCE: 2½ MILES |

DIRECTIONS TO START: BURNSALL LIES ON THE B6160 NORTH OF ILKLEY AND CAN ALSO BE REACHED FROM THE B6265 WEST OF PATELEY BRIDGE. **PARKING:** PARK IN THE INN CAR PARK OR ON THE RIVERSIDE/ROADSIDE VERGES.

This exquisitely beautiful place will make a compulsive strider of you and if your inclination is not to hare off to cover the entire Dales in a dizzy 24 hours, I'll burn my boots!

In the lee of Burnsall Fell near a curvaceous bend in the river Wharfe, Burnsall has a 12th century church, scores of pretty cottages and an impressive five-arch bridge built originally as a gift by local man Sir William Craven who went on to become Lord Mayor of London. The bridge is the centrepiece of an impromptu summer lido, but following frequent floods, it has been rebuilt many times. Our stroll begins and ends on its parapets, following the Dales Way along the river bank, through a gorge to Mill Bridge. Crossing the river on a flimsy wire and plank contraption that would have been an ideal locale for the old Tarzan films, we return through pastures, enjoying a different view with every stride.

The Red Lion

Like migrating salmon, scores of Dales visitors from the south wriggle their way past the front door of this exceptionally well-placed inn. Hard by Burnsall's picturesque bridge, its rustic charms net many a customer, its rows of outside summer tables foaming with tankards, its AA rosetted restaurant and the delightful promise of over seven miles of trout and grayling fishing proving irresistible. Once the 16th century Ferryman's Inn whose monolithic horse trough still resides near the old front door – over centuries of alterations it was easier to build round it! – this thoroughly modern but unspoilt inn has oak flooring and panelling, open fireplaces, a fascinating collection of clocks, brasses and sporting trophies and a resident cellar ghost 'who finds it amusing to turn off the beer taps and the icemaker'. Serving both bar meals and more formal candlelit dinners, the inn offers the widest choice of dining options, the menu typically including Irish oysters, chargrilled venison in season, braised shoulder of lamb, stew and dumplings, calves' liver and Dover sole with home-made chips. The inn's beers are Theakston, John Smith's and Old Speckled Hen. Opening times Monday to Saturday are 11.30 am to 11 pm. Sunday hours are 12 noon to 10.30 pm. Telephone: 01756 720204.

The Walk

① From the back car park of the inn, go left upstream along the riverside promenade and continue through various gates for about a mile on a distinctive well-signposted footpath to the pedestrian

footbridge. The path passes a crag on the far side of the river known as Wilfred Scar. Wilfred, Bishop of York, is said to have preached here prior to establishing his church in Burnsall in AD 700. Turn right over the bridge to the opposite bank.

② Walk on and go left through a gate, crossing the corner of a field, going through a second gate and turning right on a lane. Cross the Hebden Beck on a bridge and go left, following the sign 'FP To Hebden and Bank Top'. Continue between the bungalows and go through a kissing gate on a woodland edge path to a gate. Go through and continue to the footpath signs to the right of the trout hatchery.

③ Swing right on the ascending track for about 50 yards, following the sign to Hartlington Raikes. Fork left off the track before the gateway, looking out for a stepped wall crossing. Cross the wall and the apex of a narrow field and go through a wall gap by the footpath sign, following the sign direction left over a field, heading for a big tree to the right of Ranelands Farm.

The Wharfe near Burnsall (courtesy of D. Cossar)

④ Go through the gate, cross the farmyard swinging right and go through a second gate, veering left off the farm track and heading diagonally left uphill towards the field top corner. Go through the gate, veering right for 20 yards to the angle of the wall in the next field – footpath sign on other sign of the wall – and follow the sign direction, continuing uphill over a rutted track. At the brow, look out for a big tree at the field boundary and walk on to the right of the tree towards a footpath sign next to a wall. Go left here, ignoring the next gate opening, following the wall down to the corner. Cross right over the ladder stile, following the direction sign, and continue wallside for 120 yards. Go left over the

second ladder stile and follow a fence down for 250 yards to the third ladder stile. Cross, going diagonally left over the field to the direction sign.

⑤ Keeping in the field, arc right and follow the field boundaries and the sign marked 'FP Burnsall ³/₄'. Go through the gated wall gap, veering right and left at the tree over this second field, crossing a ladder stile into a third field. Keep diagonally right and head just to the right of the field corner, going through a gated wall gap and following the footpath sign into the narrow fourth field. Cross and go through a wall gap into the fifth field, veering away from the descending wall right to find a wall gap, crossing to the lane.

⑥ Cross the lane and go through a wall gap, dropping down and veering right to a ladder stile. Cross, swinging right and left to the river bank. Follow the wall down to a gated wall gap and go through to the bridge, mounting the steps left and turning right over the bridge, back to the inn.

Appletreewick
The Craven Arms

MAP REF: OS LANDRANGER 98/ OUTDOOR LEISURE 2 (GR 050602)	WALK 24	DISTANCE: 2½ MILES

DIRECTIONS TO START: APPLETREEWICK LIES EAST OF THE B6160 BETWEEN BOLTON BRIDGE (THE A59 JUNCTION) AND BURNSALL. APPROACHING FROM THE SOUTH, TURN OFF AT BARDEN BRIDGE. **PARKING:** PARK IN THE CAR PARK OPPOSITE THE INN.

With its yeomen's cottages strung out like fruit on a bough, poetically named Appletreewick – Aptrick to the locals – sits quietly in the shadow of Whithill, attentively gazing towards a bend in the river Wharfe and beyond to Simon's Seat, one of my favourite Yorkshire hills. This tiny village was once a resting place for monks journeying between Fountains Abbey and Bolton Priory and its Monks Hall or Mock Beggar Hall remains together with a building –

now the church of St John – that was the birthplace in 1548 of William Craven. An apprentice mercer in London, Craven went on to become the capital's Lord Mayor, returning to Yorkshire to restore his family home.

Gradient challenging in the first half mile, this spectacular stroll using old lead miners' tracks takes us from the village stocks to the panorama of the high moors before returning alongside gentle river banks to the village.

The Craven Arms

Granny would approve of all but the drink, this atmospheric inn preserving everything but her corsets drying by the grate. With twin bars, fire-warmed in winter – a genuine Yorkshire range with a black kettle slung over it in one – the Craven Arms is crammed with treasures from a bygone age, old brasses, pots and pans and traps covering its walls under a ceiling papered with foreign banknotes. Take a window seat and choose from a standard menu that features steak and kidney pie, lamb cutlets and Cumberland sausage or select from a specials board large on vegetarian options such as breaded jalapeno peppers and parsnip and chestnut bake. The house ales are John Smith's, Tetley, Black Sheep and Theakston. Opening times on Monday to Saturday are 11.30 am to 3 pm and 6.30 pm to 11 pm. Sunday hours are 12 noon to 3 pm and 7 pm to 10.30 pm. Telephone: 01756 720270.

Appletreewick (courtesy of D. Cossar)

The Walk

① Turn right from the inn for a few yards, and just past the stocks, turn right again on the steep track signposted to 'Dibble's Bridge'. Go through a gate and swing right, continuing to the summit. Go left through a gate, swinging left and right on a track wallside and veer left to the field corner, going through a gate.

② Turn left on a track signposted to 'Hartlington' and continue to the barn, going right through a gate, following the footpath and bridleway sign. Where the walled track ends, keep following the single wall, weaving down right and then left to the bridleway sign. Hartlington Hall is over the valley to the right – Ketel

The village stocks seen on the walk

de Hertlinton came over with the Conqueror. In his eccentric will, his ancestor Henry Hartlington who died in 1467, left his 'soul to the Omnipotent God, and his body to the church of St Wilfred at Burnsall'. Keep going forward downhill to the bridleway sign and drop down on a sunken track right to a stile, crossing to a lane. Cross and continue on a path signposted 'FP To Dales Way Path'. Swing left following a sign to 'Appletreewick' and go left of the farmhouse through a wicket gate, walking on through a gate by a barn and through a further gate, following a wall down to the river bank.

③ Turn left on the river bank for about ³/₄ mile and at the 'Appletreewick' sign go left on a path between dwarf walls (this

PLACES OF INTEREST NEARBY

New Road, the first left after leaving the village to the east, leads to the B6265. Turn right here for **Stump Cross Caverns**. These 500,000 year old caves contain a superb collection of stalactites and stalagmites. Tea room and gift shop. Open daily between April and October; weekends only during winter. Telephone: 01756 752780.

footpath is not shown on the OS map), walking on to the lane.

④ Turn right along the lane, climbing back to the inn.

A little further along the lane is another excellent country pub, the New Inn. It has its own brewery.

Hetton
The Angel

MAP REF: OS LANDRANGERS 98 AND 103/OUTDOOR LEISURE 2 (GR 963589)

WALK 25

DISTANCE: 4 MILES

DIRECTIONS TO START: THE VILLAGE OF HETTON IS ON A MINOR ROAD BETWEEN GARGRAVE AND GRASSINGTON. THE BEST ACCESS IS FROM THE EAST, USING THE B6265 AND TURNING OFF IN RYLSTONE. **PARKING:** PARK OUTSIDE THE INN OR ON THE CAR PARK OPPOSITE.

With gazebo views of the fells, tranquil Hetton is an ancient farming community, its tracks providing some of the best walking country in the National Park. Such was its isolation that the parish once housed a fever hospital. With its closure in the 1920s, the village again reverted to relative anonymity until its 600 year old inn was revived, bringing national acclaim.

This simple stroll comes with a leg warning. The marvellous food at the Angel has the properties of a spark inhibitor and leg irons combined. It is to walking what a bungee rope is to free fall. Make sure you eat after your stroll, the path leading you along old trackways to the shores of Winterburn Reservoir, returning over fields and along a classical green lane.

The Angel

By commandeering the adjacent farmyard, the proprietors of the Angel are just managing to stem the parking tide, this multiple-award-winning inn attracting customers like bees to a honey pot. Timelessly English with oak beams and open fireplaces, short of a shoe-shine boy, the Angel provides a miracle for the booted classes. Where else could you sample Ritz standard fare in your walking socks? Informal meals are served in the bar, snug and brasserie, the restaurant being reserved for special occasions. The light dining options range from terrine of parslied ham and foie gras, to warm salad of crispy duck. A more substantial standard menu includes oak smoked chicken breast panzanella, grilled calves' liver and pancetta, rib eye steak and pan roasted fillet of pork. The blackboard specials list typically features fresh fish such as pan fried skate wing, salmon fillet and haddock with queen scallops. The house ales are Black Sheep, Timothy Taylor Landlord and Tetley but wines are equally popular, the cellar bursting with vintages. Champagne and scores of other wines are available by the glass. Opening times Monday to Sunday are 12 noon to 3 pm and 6 pm to 11 pm. Telephone: 01756 730263.

The Walk

① Turn left from the inn along the lane for about 150 yards and go left, following the bridleway sign to 'Hetton Common' along a track – Moor Lane. Go through a gate and continue along the track, climbing steadily for just under 1¹/₂ miles.

If you're feeling adventurous at this point, the moorland track ahead, over Hetton Common, leads to the magnificent Gordale Scar and Malham Cove (see Walk 26).

② At the gated access to the moor, turn left, following the signpost 'BW Winterburn', going through a gate over a rough field towards Alans Plantation. Go through a gate into the wood then leave the

A typical Dales view (courtesy of D. Cossar)

PLACES OF INTEREST NEARBY

Nearby **Skipton** has a wealth of attractions including the 900 year old castle (open every day). Telephone: 01756 792442. Also the **Craven Museum** whose displays include items relating to the social history of the Dales. Open Mondays, Wednesdays, Fridays and weekends, except Sundays in winter. Telephone: 01756 706407.

Nearby **Rylstone** has a rustic pond and hidden from view, a picturesque church. Rylstone is the setting for Wordsworth's *White Doe of Rylstone*.

wood through a further gate and cross the pasture land, steering left, going through a gate and keeping straight forward towards Long Hill Farm. Go through a gate and keep the same direction, passing the farm fenceside to the field corner.

Rylstone church, near Hetton

③ Go through a gate and follow the signpost left over a very large field. The path is indeterminate for the next ¹/₂ mile, so look out for a long wall on the left – you need to keep left so that you gradually converge with this wall. Keep well left of the right-angle wall to your right and drop down towards the field corner, swinging right to a gate.

④ Go through and turn left over the small field to the corner and go left again through a gate along a green lane towards the farmhouse.

⑤ At the corner, turn left along Cross Lane, going through various gates to rejoin Moor Lane.

⑥ Turn right and retrace your steps back to the inn.

Malham
The Buck Inn

MAP REF: OS LANDRANGER 98/ OUTDOOR LEISURE 2 (GR 901628)	WALK 26	DISTANCE: 4 MILES

DIRECTIONS TO START: MALHAM, EAST OF SETTLE, CAN BE REACHED FROM THE SOUTH BY TURNING OFF THE A65 WEST OF SKIPTON AND DRIVING THROUGH AIRTON AND KIRBY MALHAM. **PARKING:** PARK AT THE INN OR IN THE PAY AND DISPLAY VISITOR CENTRE CAR PARK.

Geology in Malham takes star billing, the grandeur of its limestone canyon, waterfalls and characteristic pavements having drawn walkers for centuries. Straddling the banks of the Malham Beck, a brawling infant that issues from the amphitheatre of the fantastic Malham Cove, this ever popular village is a rambler's paradise, much of the wild and exceptionally attractive surrounding countryside having been secured for the nation by the National Trust. If your idea of a pub stroll is a five minute pavement saunter to the Bull and Bush, this excursion will seem like a bash up the Hindu Kush! But such is the route's reputation as the most scenic in the county, that its omission would be unthinkable.

The walk approaches the portals of the gigantic Gordale Scar before climbing to the most impressive natural spectacle in the whole of Yorkshire. A 300 feet high, billion ton slab of riddled and fractured limestone embracing a puny beck, Malham Cove has terrifying cliffs and an overwhelming enormity that is more than the craning neck can comprehend. Crossing the deeply fissured limestone pavement at its summit, we return by steep paths, following the beck to the village. Good boots, sure-footedness and a head for heights are all essential for this route.

The Buck Inn

Prettily situated beside a handsome bridge, the ivied Buck Inn has served countless footsore customers over the years and it is wholly fitting in this walking Mecca that it should welcome muddy boots with a passion only previously the preserve of the makers of Cherry Blossom polish. Spartan, with something of the air of a casualty department, its stone-flagged Hikers Bar is thoroughly prepared for the sloggers, and is open every day from 11 am to 11 pm. In contrast, the oak panelled, open fireplaced lounge and the elegant dining room are refinement itself. The Buck has an extensive and varied menu that includes oyster and mushroom pepperpot, lamb and spinach keema madras, mixed bean toscana, broccoli, chive and potato bake and a number of specialities such as Malham Cove – a combination of potted shrimps, prawns and mushrooms in a creamy sauce – and Malham and Masham pie – local beef cooked in Theakston ale. The ale accompaniments are Theakston, Black Sheep, Timothy Taylor and John Smith's. Daily opening times for the lounge bar are 11 am to 3 pm and 7 pm to 11 pm (10.30 pm on Sundays). Telephone: 01729 830317.

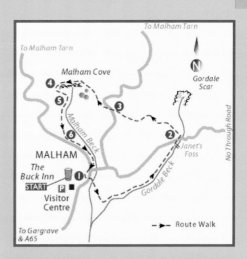

The Walk

① Go right from the inn for 20 yards then go left over a footbridge. Turn right, following a sign to 'Janet's Foss'. Continue through a gate alongside the beck, going left then right through a wicket gate, and keep on the broad and distinctive track. Go through the next wicket gate and follow the

'FP Janet's Foss' sign left for 100 yards wallside to the barn. Go left over the ladder stile and right, following a wall to a wicket gate. Go through, following the yellow arrow marker right to another wicket gate, going through and continuing on a track wallside. Cross a ladder stile and continue beckside to a further ladder stile, crossing into the National Trust reserve of Janet's Foss. (In every man and woman there is a sooty imp itching to get out. Here is a perfect opportunity to imitate the chimney sweep hero in Charles Kingsley's *Water Babies*! – he was inspired by this wonderful place. Hush . . . there's no one coming . . . strip off!) Continue to the left of the foss and go through a wicket gate to the lane.

② Turn right down the lane for 250 yards to Gordale Bridge. Go left following the sign to 'Malham Cove' over the grazing land. Go through a wicket gate and follow the wall up to a second wicket gate, crossing into a second field and right up steps to a further wicket gate, swinging left wallside on a track. Go through the next wicket gate, swinging right towards the

Malham Cove

lane, following the lane wall right for 200 yards to the signpost.

③ Go through the wall gap to the lane and turn right for 10 yards, going left over a ladder stile, following the signpost to 'Malham Cove'. Steer right on the broad track wallside to the marker post and veer left, following the signpost, swinging right to a ladder stile and left across the limestone pavement at the top of Malham Cove.

④ At the end of the pavement, weave left to a ladder stile and cross left down steps, weaving steeply down right and left through two gates to the bottom.

PLACES OF INTEREST NEARBY

No visit to Malham is complete without a visit to **Gordale Scar** and **Malham Tarn** the second largest natural lake in Yorkshire, just north of the village.

⑤ Turn right on the broad path, continuing through two gates to the lane.

⑥ Turn left into the village. At the Beck Hall sign, leave the lane, going through a gate onto a path alongside Malham Beck, and continue beckside almost back to the inn. Fork right across the road to the starting point.

Settle
The Golden Lion

<table>
<tr><td>MAP REF: OS LANDRANGER 98/
OUTDOOR LEISURE 2 (GR 819637)</td><td>WALK 27</td><td>DISTANCE: 4 MILES</td></tr>
</table>

DIRECTIONS TO START: SETTLE IS LOCATED OFF THE A65 SKIPTON-KENDAL TRUNK ROAD. **PARKING:** PARK IN THE CENTRE OF SETTLE – IN THE SHAMBLES – OR ON THE PAY AND DISPLAY FACILITY A FEW HUNDRED YARDS NORTH-WEST NEAR THE RAILWAY VIADUCT.

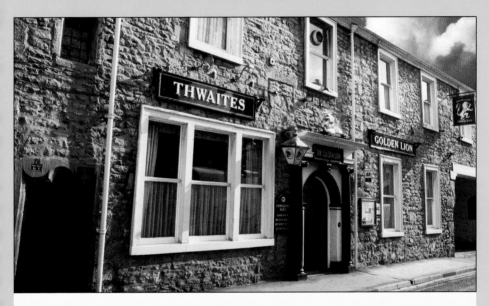

Squeezed into the neck of Ribblesdale with rough scars outreaching its chimneys, Settle is a frontier town where you check your ammunition before setting out into the unknown. Still a place of bustle despite the opening of a new bypass, the town is clustered around the Shambles – a sort of rustic piazza – other curious buildings like the 17th century Folly and the Ye Olde Naked Man Café exciting visitor interest. Beneath the frowning Castleberg Crag, the town has long been identified with the surrounding scars and caves, this memorable walk taking us to the famous Victoria Cave. Discovered in the year of Queen Victoria's Coronation, it has yielded mammoth, elephant, hippopotamus and hyena bones, together with human deposits from the Stone Age. Like the circuit of Malham Cove on page 83, this taxing but unmissable walk discovers petrified seas of limestone – features that so typify the Yorkshire Dales.

The Golden Lion

Built around 1640 as a coaching inn, the commodious, almost cavernous Golden Lion has two attractive bars, one with a splendid log-burning hearth of roast ox size. Popular with locals and just a stride from the Shambles, it offers a good blackboard selection of bar meals such as lamb cutlets, tenderloin of pork, grilled salmon, crispy prawns and chicken and liver terrine, together with more exotic dishes in its 70 seater restaurant. The house ales are exclusively from the local Thwaites Brewery. Opening times Monday to Saturday are 11 am to 11 pm. Sunday hours are 12 noon to 3 pm and 7 pm to 10.30 pm. Telephone: 01759 822203.

The Walk

① Turn right from the inn to the Shambles, walk across the parking area and go right up the steep Constitution Hill. At the top of the hill, go left along the lane to the telegraph pole numbered 463722 and follow the Pennine Bridleway signed track right between the drystone walls, climbing up to a narrow copse. Go through a gate by a roofless barn and continue wallside for 150 yards.

② Go right, following a public footpath sign to Malham, climbing steeply uphill wallside. Veer left away from the wall and continue climbing on the green track to the right of Blua Crags. Go through a gate opening and keep wallside on the flat path (notice the caves in the crags to the left). Where the route forks, go left keeping wallside. Cross the 90° angle line of a broken wall (yellow marker spot on wall) and follow the track as it veers off right of the crags and swing right to the wall corner opposite the mouth of the cave. Go left 60 yards to a public footpath sign and, keeping the same direction, drop down following the wall. Cross a ladder stile and follow the wall down passing the rusted metal plates. Go through the gate opening.

③ Go left up the narrow valley between the scars veering away from the wall on a well-defined stony track. Merge with a green track and steer right to the corner of a wall (yellow marker spot on wall). Follow the wall down swinging right uphill to a gate. Go through and follow the wall down, passing Victoria Cave (a scrambling path leads up to its mouth where there is an information board). As well as mounds of prehistoric animal bones, the cave has also yielded beads, brooches, fish harpoons, pottery and Roman coins. Walk on for about 400 yards and go through a kissing

PLACES OF INTEREST NEARBY

The town of **Settle** is well worth further exploration. It has a market on Tuesdays.

Warrendale Knots near Settle

gate, swinging left to the 'Victoria Cave' sign.

④ Go left through a gate on a track, swinging right and left and right again alongside a wood to the road.

⑤ Go immediately left on the bend through a gate, following the 'BW Settle 2' sign. Keep on the green track below the wood and drop down right towards a copse. Go through a gate, continuing on a stony track to another gate, going through along a green track and dropping down right to a gate. Go through and follow the wall down, continuing through the next gate to the outward route. Follow this back to Settle and the inn.

Giggleswick
The Black Horse

MAP REF: OS LANDRANGER 98/ OUTDOOR LEISURE 2 (GR 813641)

WALK 28

DISTANCE: 3 MILES

DIRECTIONS TO START: GIGGLESWICK IS A NEIGHBOUR OF SETTLE, JUST OFF THE A65 SKIPTON-KENDAL ROAD. **PARKING:** PARK IN THE INN'S REAR CAR PARK. ALTERNATIVELY, USE THE PARKING AREA AT THE RATHMELL ROAD JUNCTION – FIRST LEFT PAST THE CHURCH, GOING WEST.

Is this a suburb of Knotty Ash or a summer retreat for Doddy and his Diddymen? Or did the man who named this rather grand little village have a tattifilereous sense of humour? With its own railway station, a distinguished public school, a trunk road passing its front door and the whole of glorious Ribblesdale on its doorstep, 'Gigel's village' has much to commend it. Built around the church of St Alkelda which has a market cross outside its gate, the village, with its gaggle of interesting date-stoned cottages clustered round the Tems Beck, is internationally known for its excellent school founded in 1553. This Dales foray along the Ribble Way takes us to the hamlet of Stackhouse and back along the foot of scree slopes crowned with intriguingly-named features like Kelcow Caves, Nevison's Nick and Schoolboys Tower. I bet plenty of names have gone in the truants' book after visits to that!

The Black Horse

Such is its proximity to the village church and its ecclesiastical architecture that you might expect only communion wine in this establishment. But fear not, the local vicar enjoys the juice of malt along with the rest of us in this unique old coaching inn dating from 1663. Filled with interesting treasures – including two wall mounted pin-ball machines from the 1950s, rustic tools, brasses and antique pictures – it has twin bars with pew seats and a small dining room. Bolstered by weekly specials, the robust standard menu features steak and ale pie, chicken liver with spicy stuffed mushrooms, barbecue pork, minted lamb and fresh fish. Four ales are on tap – Timothy Taylor, Tetley, Theakston and John Smith's. Opening times on Monday are 5.30 pm to 11 pm and on Tuesday to Friday 12 noon to 2.30 pm and 5.30 pm to 11 pm. Saturday and Sunday hours are 12 noon to 11 pm (10.30 pm on Sundays). Telephone: 01729 822506.

The Walk

① Leaving the front door of the inn, walk to the village cross and go left, turning left again up Belle Hill to the B6480. Cross the road and go right on the footway, walking on past the swimming pool towards the river bridge.

② Go left just before the bridge and the Settle sign on a path, swinging left riverside along the topside of the playing field. Keep arcing left for about 60 yards between a wall and a fence and go right, through a wall gap, crossing a meadow to a second wall gap. Go through, continuing wallside on a bank, crossing a fence and mounting steps, keeping forward fenceside to a wall gap. Go through into a meadow and veer diagonally left to a gated wall gap and a sign.

③ Cross the lane, go right for 10 yards and then left into a sloping field through a wall gap for about 20 yards and swing right, following a line parallel with the lane towards the bottom of the wood. Converge with the wall right and fork left uphill on a track, following the sign to 'Feizor'. Keep climbing to the 'Stackhouse Lane/Stainforth/Feizor' sign and follow the Feizor route left, walking uphill and on

PLACES OF INTEREST NEARBY

Go into Settle and turn left on the B6479 towards Horton-in-Ribblesdale to reach the **Watershed Mill Visitor Centre**. Based on a refurbished 19th century cotton mill, this complex has 52 craft shops and a coffee shop. Open daily. Telephone: 01729 825111/825539.

The Ribble near Stainforth

over a field to a ladder stile. Do not climb, but go left along the wall for 130 yards. Just west of here is the impressive Giggleswick Scar. These precipitous limestone crags are part of the Craven Fault. At the foot of the scar is the curious site of the Ebbing and Flowing Well.

④ Turn left at the next ladder stile and cross the field corner, heading for the topside of the wood, following the wall down to a third ladder stile. Cross right and go left on a path, veering right away from the line of the wall. Continue through the bracken, dropping down on the broad, snaking path and go through a gate, swinging left to the wood. Go left through the gate into the wood on a track and drop down, continuing on a path into the residential area. Keep going forward on The Mains to the road. Turn right, cross the B6480 and go left back down Belle Hill, turning right to return to the inn.

Embsay
The Elm Tree

MAP REF: OS LANDRANGERS 103 AND 104/OUTDOOR LEISURE 2 (GR 008538)

WALK 29

DISTANCE: 3½ MILES

DIRECTIONS TO START: EMBSAY LIES NORTH-EAST OF SKIPTON, ONE MILE FROM THE A59 BYPASS. **PARKING:** PARK EITHER IN THE PUB'S REAR CAR PARK OR IN THE ADJACENT (FREE) VISITORS' CAR PARK.

This old mill town is dominated by its crag, whose shadow once fell on an Augustinian priory founded around 1120. The gatehouse to thousands of acres of moors and fells with captivating names like Punchbowl and Ladle, Deer Gallows Ridge, The Whams, Onion Hill and Dolly Rogin, it is an exhilarating place with something of the air of a rain forest clearing. Part the canopy, get one whiff of the heather and you will be up and away! Using quiet lanes and paths, this stroll takes us to the top of Embsay Crag where we will enjoy the panoramic views before returning to the town alongside a reservoir and an old mill goit.

The Elm Tree

In the pretty Elm Tree Square, this inviting stone-built pub has a spacious bar sparkling with brass and stained glass and a separate pewed dining area. The standard menu features beef and ale cobbler, turkey and ham pie, gammon steak, haddock and cheese and broccoli bake. A daily specials board offers alternative dishes such as vegetable and Stilton crumble, chicken, bacon and leek pie and pork and bean casserole, the wide choice of food being matched by an equally varied selection of rotating guest ales, the list typically including Goose Eye, Old Speckled Hen, Flowers, Cains and Caledonian. Opening times Monday to Saturday are 11.30 am to 3 pm and 5.30 pm to 11 pm. Sunday hours are 12 noon to 3 pm and 7 pm to 10.30 pm. Telephone: 01756 790717.

The Walk

① Turn left from the pub and go left through the car park and through a gate, crossing a field right to the corner. Go

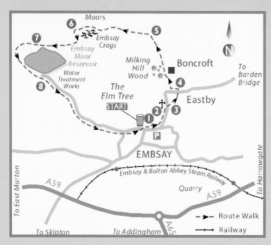

PLACES OF INTEREST NEARBY
The **Embsay Steam Railway** operates from the town, linking Embsay with Bolton Abbey. Trains run every Sunday throughout the year and on weekends from Easter until the end of October. Tuesdays in May, June, early July and September. Daily from mid July until the end of August. Speaking timetable: 01756 795189. General enquiries: 01756 794727. In nearby **Skipton** see one of the best preserved medieval castles in England. Open every day. Telephone: 01756 792442.

through a wall gap and turn right on a path, going through a second wall gap and diagonally left over a second field to the corner. Go through a kissing gate to the lane.

② Turn left using the footway and pass the church of St Mary Virgin. At the churchyard corner, cross the road right.

③ Go through a wicket gate, following a footpath sign, and cross two fields, going through a final gate and swinging left to the lane. Turn left for about 300 yards.

④ Turn right uphill, following the bridleway sign to 'Embsay Crag'. Cross the cattle grid and swing left, climbing up to the buildings at Boncroft and going left through a gate, following the bridleway sign. Pass Milking Hill Wood on the left and continue ascending to a gate.

⑤ Go through and left, following the sign and the blue tipped posts along the distinctive path through the bracken, weaving right and left and up to the top of the crag.

Embsay railway station (courtesy of R. Hartley)

⑥ Drop off the crag right and descend, gradually swinging left towards the dam wall. Fork right to the blue tipped post, heading for the top of the reservoir, and fork right again, dropping down to the reservoir boundary wall.

⑦ Turn right wallside and cross the bridge and swing right to the signpost, going left on a path to a stile. Cross and turn left on a track passing the reservoir to the sailing club.

⑧ Turn left on the lane (few vehicles – no through road) and swing right by the water works, going round the next bend left alongside the goit ponds. Continue on Pasture Road back to the pub.

Bolton Bridge
The Devonshire Arms Hotel

MAP REF: OS LANDRANGER 104/ OUTDOOR LEISURE 2 (GR 071531)

WALK 30

DISTANCE: 2 MILES

DIRECTIONS TO START: BOLTON BRIDGE NEAR BOLTON ABBEY IS JUST OFF THE A59 HARROGATE-SKIPTON ROAD. **PARKING:** PARK IN THE HOTEL CAR PARK OR IN THE PAY AND DISPLAY FACILITY TO THE NORTH OF THE HOTEL.

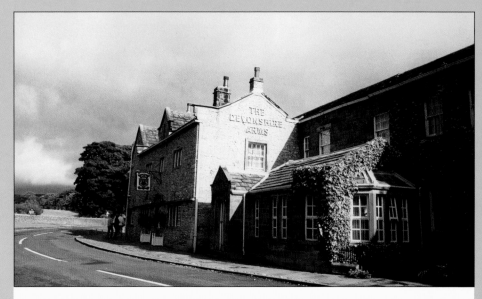

Bypassed, and made redundant by a re-routed A59, old Bolton Bridge melts into a landscape made famous by Turner, his painting of the skeletal Augustinian priory upstream being one of the most beautiful canvases in England. Three miles from the chilling cauldron of water known as the Strid is a more placid stretch of river, the Strand, echoing its London namesake in a natural opulence and a romantic history that makes this stroll the most compelling in the National Park. A simple amble that in dry weather can be almost accomplished in carpet slippers, it follows the banks of the Wharfe to Bolton Hall and the priory. Founded in 1151, this retreat of the Black Canons is raised on a promontory above a delectable sweep in the river, the rapturous eye rising in a symphonic cadence of views from its scalloped capitals to the wooded crags above the river and beyond to the moors and glens of Barden Fell. An intrinsic part of the priory is a surviving church. We return over a pedestrian bridge – forget the slippers and use the alternative stepping stones – continuing along a cliff top path via Priors Pool back to the bridge.

The Devonshire Arms Hotel

Owned by the Duke of Devonshire since 1773, this elegant country house hotel is appointed to the very highest standards, its opulence enhanced by many paintings and items of furniture borrowed from the Devonshire family seat at Chatsworth House. For the casual visitor it offers a bridge and ultra modern brasserie bar with the accent on light meals such as smoked salmon, roast aubergine with a pesto crust and skewered king prawns and chicken although more robust appetites can contemplate the whole hog in the Burlington Restaurant. Complementing the food the hotel has an extensive wine list and serves vintages by the glass. The brasserie bar is open Monday to Wednesday from 12 noon to 3 pm and 6.30 pm to 11 pm and Thursday to Sunday from 12 noon to 11 pm (10.30 pm on Sunday). Telephone: 01756 710441.

PLACES OF INTEREST NEARBY

Just up the road is the **Bolton Abbey Estate** whose Strid Wood, extensive nature trails and Cavendish Pavilion – good refreshments – are open to the public. A car parking charge is payable. Open all year. Telephone: 01756 710533.

The Walk

① Turn left from the hotel and walk on the footway, swinging left and following the closed road to the old bridge. Turn left onto the water meadows, following the signpost 'FP Bolton Priory'. Follow the path left towards the priory and explore the ruins – free admittance. An interpretation board in the grounds refers to the canons whose triple vow was to poverty, chastity and obedience. The priory was suppressed in 1539. Drop down to the bridge and cross.

② Swing left and go right up the steep bank to the footpath signs, turning right on the cliff track signposted to 'Bolton

Barden Bridge – this elegant structure is the next road crossing upstream of Bolton Bridge.

Bolton Priory

Bridge'. Go left over a stile and continue beside the fence, turning right over a stile into a second field. Follow a fence down, going right and left downhill to a stile. Cross and follow a footpath sign into a third field over a ditch. Go through a gate into a fourth field and follow the path left uphill, veering to the right of the next gate entrance, crossing a stile into a fifth field and swinging right fenceside to the right of a barn. Cross a stile and walk on between the buildings to the road, turning right to the old bridge. Cross and return to the hotel.